BARR FLIES

BARR FLIES

How to Tie and Fish
the Copper John, the Barr Emerger
and Dozens of Other Patterns,
Variations and Rigs

JOHN S. BARR

FLY PHOTOGRAPHY BY
CHARLIE CRAVEN

STACKPOLE
BOOKS

Published by
STACKPOLE BOOKS
5067 Ritter Road
Mechanicsburg, PA 17055
www.stackpolebooks.com

Printed in China

First edition

10 9 8 7 6 5 4 3 2

Illustrations by Dave Hall

Library of Congress Cataloging-in-Publication Data

Barr, John, 1944–
  Barr flies : how to tie and fish the Copper John, the Barr Emerger, and dozens of other
patterns, variations, and rigs / John Barr. — 1st ed.
      p. cm.
  Includes index.
  ISBN-13: 978-0-8117-0236-2
  ISBN-10: 0-8117-0236-7
  ISBN-13: 978-0-8117-0276-8 (limited ed.)
  ISBN-10: 0-8117-0276-6 (limited ed.)
  1. Fly tying. I. Title.

SH451.B277 2007
688.7'9124—dc22
                                                          2006038362

*To my wife Jeanne,
my son Jonathan,
and my daughter Jessica.*

CONTENTS

ACKNOWLEDGMENTS

I would be remiss if I did not start with my longtime friend Van Rollo, the premier fly-fishing manufacturers' rep in the country and owner of Mountain Sports in Boulder, Colorado. Almost twenty years ago he urged me to submit some fly samples to Umpqua Feather Merchants, the number one producer of flies in the world. In 1970, Umpqua started a program that paid a royalty to fly tiers for their original patterns. Van convinced me to send in some of my patterns to Umpqua, and they picked up a couple of them. That was the moment that eventually enabled me to combine my lifelong passion for fly fishing with the business side of the fly industry.

As the years progressed and my patterns became successful, other manufacturers took notice, and today I can proudly say that I am associated with the most elite manufacturers in the industry. I cannot thank them enough for their support.

I would like to thank Judith Schnell, Publisher and Vice President of Stackpole Books, for giving me the opportunity to write this book, and Jay Nichols, former Managing Editor of *Fly Fisherman* magazine, for his encouragement and support throughout the process. Jay now owns his own publishing business, Headwater Books. I owe a great deal to John Randolph, Editor and Publisher of *Fly Fisherman* magazine, for publishing several of my articles, which gave me the confidence to tackle writing a book.

Thanks to Charlie Craven for spending countless hours taking the exquisite fly-tying photos and writing the tutorials. Thanks to Landon Mayer who spent lots of time taking onstream photos of fish. The fishing could be really hot, but Landon would quit fishing and take his time to compose the shots and get the lighting just right.

I would like to thank the Umpqua Feather Merchant reps and the fly shops throughout the country, without whose support this book never would have been possible. I would also like to thank Umpqua's personnel who have supported me all of these years.

Lastly, I would like to thank all of those with whom I've crossed paths in the world of fly fishing—many are lifelong friends. There is not room to name them all, but every one is special to me.

FOREWORD

The year was 1978, notable for the Camp David peace accord, the death of two popes, and the birth of history's first test-tube baby. People still sent letters by mail and hardly anyone used fly rods in pursuit of northern pike.

My personal epiphany for pike had come the previous year on Canada's Great Slave Lake, where two anglers from Calgary arrived with large flies made from clumps of chicken feathers wrapped irregularly around a hook. Even with such rudimentary implements, the result was spectacular. A visitor from the States never had reason to take spinning tackle north again.

A second discovery, later that same season, revealed that pike had taken hold in several reservoirs in Colorado. Naturally, I had to blab about this, along with the prospect for fly fishing, in my column in the *Denver Post,* a common disease among outdoor writers. Only this time, things turned out all for the best.

That's when the letter arrived, fairly oozing questions. Just where might these toothy monsters be found? In what type of water? Then finally, inevitably, what kind of flies? A letterhead proclaimed the sender to be someone from Boulder named John Barr. I dialed the phone number and found myself immersed in conversation with someone with unbridled passion for the more unusual aspects of the fly sport. The exchange was riveting. On a busy day, I simply couldn't put down the phone.

A second envelope, about a week later, bulged with something much more tangible. What spilled onto my desk was a remarkable arrangement of fur, feathers, and tinsel that I imagined to be the finest flies ever designed exclusively with northern pike in mind. I ached to get them in the water.

Predictably, Barr beat me to it. In a state of high excitement, he told of landing a 25-pounder, surely the largest pike ever caught in the state at the time. It was a signal event in a string of successes that were to become commonplace for the man who arguably ranks as America's most successful designer of commercially distributed flies.

With remarkable regularity, he cranks out patterns that dazzle with a rare combination of form and function, clever concoctions that don't spend much time loitering in the fly shop. Barr's flies catch fishermen because they also catch fish.

Moreover, they catch fish in large part because that's precisely what Barr was doing when the notion for the fly came to him. John doesn't do knock-offs of existing patterns or expand on someone else's ideas. Virtually all those concepts creep intuitively into his awareness while trying to resolve some standoff with a persnickety trout.

Take, for example, that day on Nelson's Spring Creek in Montana, one of those famous trout emporiums where fish take perverse satisfaction in heaping embarrassment upon even the most accomplished anglers—usually in front of friends.

Barr's frustration that day stuck in his craw, rattled around in his brain, and eventually crept out through his fingertips in the form of the Barr Emerger. Whether styled to imitate the Pale Morning Dun or Blue-Winged Olive, tied flashback or bead-head, this pattern remains unsurpassed for the majority of western mayfly situations.

A similarly perceived need for a nymph that combined the elements of attraction and rapid sink while retaining a suggestive profile caused him a decade ago to launch his design of the Copper John, which evolved into the most popular fly of the millennium. You'll find some version of the pattern in nearly every fly box, simply because it puts fish on the line.

From that basic design, Barr has produced a number of equally effective variations, along with a concept that continues to alter the way many fly fishers approach trout with nymphs. John didn't invent the multiple-fly rig. His contribution lies in the way he uses the Copper John as centerpiece of a three-fly system that optimizes fish-catching potential.

He calls this setup the Hopper-Copper-Dropper. It starts with the B/C Hopper, a large closed-cell foam creation he fashioned with Denver tying guru Charlie Craven. The Hopper, which might float an anvil, serves both as indicator and a juicy morsel that often produces splashy strikes.

Next comes a Copper John, that anchor and attention-getter. Trout that don't bite the Copper get hooked on the dropper, typically a smaller nymph that imitates the prevailing insect of the day. When it comes to pulling trout from a river, you'd have to use a gill net to do better.

Barr's successes aren't limited to streams. He spends considerable time on the saltwater flats, out in the deep blue, and paddling around warmwater ponds for bass— the inspiration for his latest success, a streamer he calls, appropriately, the Meat Whistle.

At this writing, twenty-three of Barr's patterns are listed in the Umpqua Feather Merchants catalog, stamping him among the nation's leading contract tiers.

We already know most of these patterns, having used many in pursuit of an assortment of fish. Now, for the first time, we are allowed to examine them collectively and in full detail in John's first book.

This anthology is long past due, but more than worth the wait. By the time you read this, John Barr likely will have fashioned several more successful patterns. Can a second book be far away?

—CHARLIE MEYERS

PREFACE

My fly-tying journey started in a garage many years ago when I was five or six years old. I went next door to say hello to my friend Bud Owens, who was a janitor at the Naval Base in Seattle where I lived. He was sitting at a card table in his garage doing something with his hands.

Bud was at his vise, which was most likely a Thompson, and he had a little pile of Gray-Hackle Peacocks on the table next to him, and was in the process of tying another one. When I asked him what he was doing, he told me that he was tying some flies. At the time I didn't know what a fly was, but I remember the inexplicable energy that surged through my body while I was looking at that clump of flies.

My affair with flies and fly tying started that afternoon. My first flies were tied on bent nails and were dressed with strips of a bed sheet that I dyed with raspberries from our garden. I didn't fish with these creations, but I was having a good time. I progressed from there to tying actual flies on hooks. My dad took me down to Patrick's Fly Shop in Seattle, and Roy Patrick set me up with the basics, including a spiral-bound pattern book, the name of which I've long forgotten. Bud Owens taught me the fundamentals.

As I recall, my first fly, which was from the pattern book, was called a Dead Chicken, if you can believe it. The Dead Chicken was a wet fly, and it had a red rooster fiber tail, a yellow chenille body, and a grizzly hackle. I am not sure if I ever caught a fish on it. I tied my first "original" pattern when I was around eight or nine. I called it the Log. Our family used to vacation in northern California at my great uncle "Cedar" Ed's logging camp. I sold a dozen Logs to a logger for three dollars. They were the first and last flies that I ever personally sold.

A small stream called Willow Creek flowed in front of the cabin where we stayed, and it was loaded with two- to five-inch rainbows. My first fly rod was one of the old telescopic metal ones that extended from two feet to eight or nine feet long and probably weighed around a pound. I can't remember what kind of reel, line, and leader I used, but I'm sure they were all equally as cumbersome. I fished nothing but dry flies. When a trout took the fly, I often set the hook so hard the trout

Every day onstream is an opportunity to learn something about the fish, the food they feed on, and the surroundings in which they live. Over the years, I have simplified my system for matching the hatch, and I share this system in this book.
LANDON MAYER

would land in one of the many bushes along the bank, where some of them stayed along with my fly and leader. The ones that landed on the ground promptly got whacked and strung on a V-shaped branch to be eaten later.

When I was twelve, we moved to San Jose, California. Within biking distance of our house, there were a number of gravel pits full of crappies and bluegills. It was

The Log (above) was the first, and the last, fly that I ever personally sold. CHARLIE CRAVEN

in these ponds that I tested another one of my original patterns—a tuft of white marabou on a size 10 dry-fly hook, with a split shot pinched right behind the hook eye. That pattern was lethal on the crappies and bluegills. The days of being a dry fly purist were officially over.

As I started to branch out in my fly fishing, I began fishing the Merced River in Yosemite National Park and streams and lakes throughout the Sierras. My favorite flies were a brown Bivisable, a hairwing Western Coachman, and a Western Bucktail. I thought I was getting pretty good until I was put in my place while fishing the Merced with my football coach, Bob Berry, and his two sons. Bob was a pretty intimidating figure, and he never held back when criticism was warranted. That evening there were fish rising everywhere. Bob was strictly a worm fisherman and could not exactly match the hatch. I was the only one hooking any fish, but not commensurate with the number of fish rising. I overheard Bob say to one of his kids, "Can you imagine what a good fly fisherman could do right now?" I was crushed, but it made me more determined than ever to improve my skills. My game is better now than back then, but I continue to learn something every time I go fishing.

We live in a great time for fly fishing. Never before have there been so many innovative, effective patterns to choose from. However, this is both a blessing and a curse for fly fishers. With the thousands of patterns available, how do you decide on which ones to put in your box? With this book I hope to simplify that dilemma.

I don't try to cover every single aquatic insect and its imitations in this book. Instead, I share with you my patterns representing the aquatic insects that provide a significant part of the diet for trout found from the east coast to the west coast. They are all proven patterns that,

when used at an appropriate time with a good presentation, will catch fish. I chose to only include my fly patterns in this book—not because they are the best ones or the only ones that I think you should fish with—but they are the ones that I know best.

There are many correct ways to accomplish a goal in life, and the same holds true for fly fishing. Nothing is etched in stone. Numerous patterns are effective for each fishing situation. For example, during a *Baetis* hatch a number of different dun and emerger patterns work. But because you cannot carry every pattern, you need to distill your patterns into a workable number that will cover most of the scenarios that you can expect to encounter. The flies in this book are the patterns that I carry with me at all times. This year I will catch most of my fish on these patterns. You need to have flies that you have confidence in for a given situation. The flies in this book are a compilation of my "confidence" patterns.

The primary focus of this book is to discuss the various fly patterns that I have designed over the past thirty years. I will discuss how and why I invented the fly patterns, when and how to fish them, and approaches that I have developed over many years of on-the-water experience. I will share thoughts on subjects ranging from trout behavior to tackle and try to provide practical information about trout and aquatic insect behavior, and what it takes to have a successful, enjoyable day of angling on streams, rivers, and still waters. I hope you enjoy reading it and learning how to tie my favorite patterns via the step-by-step tutorials and brilliant photography by Charlie Craven, owner of Charlie's Fly Box in Arvada, Colorado.

CHAPTER 1

Original Copper John

In the early 1990s, my good friend Jackson Streit introduced me to an approach to trout fishing that would forever change the way I fished. We launched the boat at 8:30 A.M. on the Colorado River at State Bridge, Colorado, and planned to complete our float about eight miles downriver. As we approached one of Jackson's favorite runs, he skillfully rowed the boat to the far side of the river, and we drifted down the bank so we wouldn't spook the fish. We eddied out at the tail of the run and dropped anchor.

The run was a fishy-looking, gentle, two- to four-foot-deep riffle about fifty yards long. We started at the tail, planning to work our way to the head. Jackson walked about forty feet above me, and we began casting. We were both fishing early prototype versions of the B/C Hopper. Quickly, Jackson was tight to a fish. As he was landing the bright, 16-inch rainbow, I noticed that the Hopper pattern was dangling above the water's surface.

I couldn't imagine how he could have hooked the fish if he didn't hook it on the Hopper, and I asked him what on earth was going on. He said he was fishing two flies—a Hopper-Dropper—and that the fish was hooked on a nymph trailing off the bend of the Hopper. After watching Jackson land that fish, and having him explain how to rig up the tandem flies, I immediately attached two feet of tippet to the hook bend and tied a weighted golden stone nymph to the tippet. I cast the two flies upstream, and the first two or three times my Hopper went under I cursed it for not floating well. I was waiting for a fish to take the Hopper. Jackson started laughing and said that a fish taking the nymph beneath the Hopper was making it sink. I had forgotten that there was a nymph below the Hopper. From that moment on, whenever my Hopper sinks, I set.

Spending time that day fishing with this highly effective method changed the way I fly-fished. Wherever it is legal, I always fish a combination of flies, whether it is two or three nymphs, a dry fly and nymphs, two drys, or two streamers.

CHARLIE CRAVEN

COPPER JOHN
(Copper)

Hook:	Size 10–18 Tiemco 5262
Bead:	Gold
Weight:	Lead wire
Thread:	Black 70-denier Ultra Thread
Tail:	Brown goose biots
Abdomen:	Copper Ultra Wire
Wing case:	Black Thin Skin and pearl Flashabou covered with 30-minute epoxy
Thorax:	Peacock herl
Legs:	Mottled brown hen back

BAIT AND SWITCH

Fishing a nymph off the bend of a dry fly was a fun and productive way to fish, but I wanted to take it to the next level: if I could fish one nymph under a large dry fly, why not try two? My thought was to have a fast-sinking, attractor fly as the first fly and a more realistic, unweighted pattern such as a caddis pupa or emerging mayfly attached to it that represented the prevailing insect activity.

1

The Colorado River downstream from the State Bridge access. ROSS PURNELL

After three years of experimenting, I came up with the Copper John, a fly designed with the sole purpose of sinking quickly and attracting a fish's attention to the more natural-looking pattern that trailed behind it. Though it is shaped roughly like a mayfly or stonefly nymph, I did not intend for the Copper John to represent any particular aquatic insect. After experimenting with the pattern in different combinations, I found that it was an effective pattern in its own right. It is flashy and doesn't look nearly as natural as the flies I often fish behind it, but the fish loved it. I think they hit the fly just because it catches their attention, resulting in what conventional tackle fishermen call a reaction strike—such as when a bass strikes a large, crazy-looking spinnerbait that doesn't look like anything that lives in the water.

The Copper John went through several design changes over a period of about three years beginning in 1993. The early patterns caught fish, but I didn't consider it finished until 1996. After trying numerous hook styles, I settled on the Tiemco 5262, a 2XL, 2X heavy hook. (For those new to fly tying, this simply means a hook with a shank that is twice as long as a standard dry-fly hook, and wire that's twice as heavy.) I tried many hook styles, but the proportions just came out the best on the Tiemco 5262, and it was a good strong hook.

In the first version, I wrapped natural-colored copper wire on the hook shank to form the abdomen. Because the fly had no underbody, the abdomen didn't have any taper. The original pattern's tail and legs were Hungarian partridge and the thorax was wrapped peacock herl with

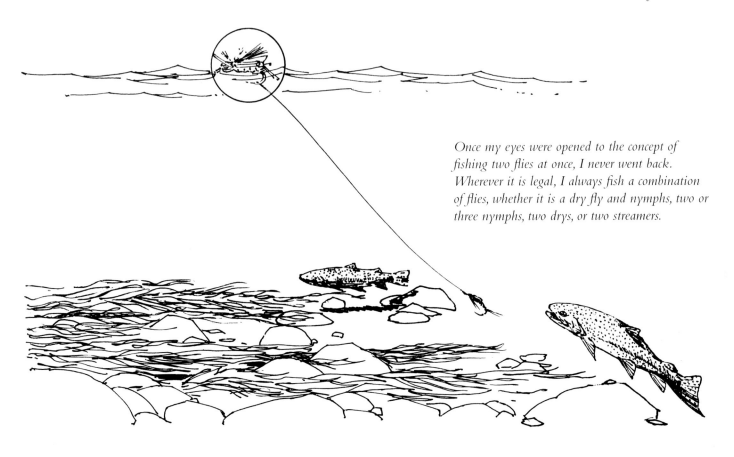

Once my eyes were opened to the concept of fishing two flies at once, I never went back. Wherever it is legal, I always fish a combination of flies, whether it is a dry fly and nymphs, two or three nymphs, two drys, or two streamers.

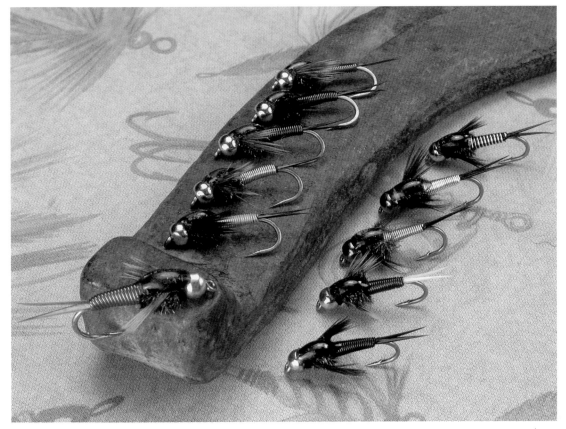

You can tie the Copper John in a wide range of colors, including (from top left to right) red, blue, green, copper, chartreuse, black, wine, pink, silver, and zebra. If I was limited to three sizes and four colors, I would carry sizes 14–18 in natural copper, red, chartreuse, and black.

The Copper John has revolutionized the way I fly-fish. I discovered that the fast-sinking fly was effective for not only getting other nymphs to the bottom quickly, but also for catching its share of fish. LANDON MAYER

an epoxied turkey quill wing case. I first saw epoxy used to coat wing cases years ago on a Hal Jansen's Callibaetis nymph pattern. The epoxy may give off a little glow that many emerging nymphs and pupae exhibit. I do not know if the epoxy makes the fly more effective, but it sure gives the fly curb appeal.

When Wapsi introduced Thin Skin, I began to use that instead of turkey quill for the wing case. Thin Skin is a versatile synthetic material that comes in sheets and can be used for wing pads, wing cases, and backs on nymphs. Thin Skin is durable, easy to work with, more readily available than turkey, and accepts the epoxy coating better than the turkey. The first layer of epoxy I used soaked into the turkey feather and a second coat was required.

I also changed the materials for the tail and legs. The partridge wasn't very durable, so I switched from hen-

back feathers to fibers for the legs and to goose biots for the tail. The hen-back fibers were durable and came in a variety of mottled colors.

To make the fly sink faster, I wrapped lead wire on the hook under the thorax. I chose the metal bead, lead, wire abdomen, and slim profile to achieve the fastest sink rate possible. I added a tapered thread underbody so the abdomen had a nice taper when the wire was wrapped over it. The fly was almost where I wanted it. The final piece was put into place when artist Dave Hall suggested pulling a single piece of pearl Flashabou over the top of the Thin Skin before applying the epoxy. The pattern was finished.

At first I only tied the fly in natural copper. Michael White, owner of Blue Ribbon Sales, who lives in Boulder, Colorado, suggested I try red and green wire. It took me a few years to try the red and green, which turned out to be productive colors. In spring 2001, Wapsi introduced Ultra Wire, a tarnish-proof wire available in a wide assortment of colors. The original copper-colored fly now shared space in my fly box with Copper Johns tied in red, green, chartreuse, silver, wine, zebra (black and silver), black, blue, and hot pink.

COLORS

There are a lot of wire colors available today, and many anglers ask me what color of fly to use and when to fish them. I catch fish on all of the colors, but if I had to choose three sizes and four colors, I would carry sizes 14–18 in natural copper, red, chartreuse, and black.

In some situations, a particular color is more effective than others. For instance, a 16 red Copper John is lethal when there have been Pale Morning Duns (PMDs) or yellow sallies hatching. (On the streams that I fish, these two insects often hatch together.) I trail a 16 Flashback PMD Emerger off the bend of the red Copper John, and this combination has worked in so many different rivers that I don't even think about using any other patterns during PMD time.

In the spring when there are a lot of caddis hatching (almost always green-olive larvae and pupae), my first choice is either green or chartreuse. Size 18–22 black patterns make excellent *Baetis* nymph imitations and can be good choices if Tricos have been hatching. If the Trico hatch has been in full force, the trout will have seen many drowned spinners whose prominent feature is the black body, and the small black Copper John can be taken as a drowned Trico spinner. A size 12 black Copper John is a good green drake or stonefly nymph. In lakes my go-to colors are sizes 14–18 red (many midge larvae are red and are often larger than river midges), sizes 14–18 chartreuse (to represent damselfly nymphs or just because it seems all

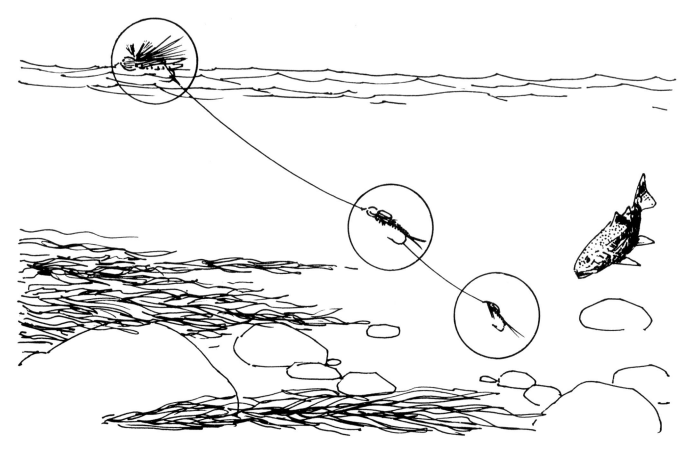

When fishing the Hopper-Copper-Dropper (HCD), the Copper John is always first in line under the floating fly. I use a tapered 7½-foot 3X regular mono leader with a heavy butt section to the B/C Hopper, 2 to 4 feet (length varies with water depth) of 4X fluorocarbon to the Copper John, and about 12 inches of 5X fluorocarbon tippet to the dropper. This progression helps turn over the flies and reduce tangles.

fish like chartreuse), and sizes 14–18 zebra (black and silver). Many midge pupae have contrasting light and dark bands on their bodies. One of my good friends, Van Rollo, swears by blue and zebra for river fishing.

HOW TO FISH THE COPPER JOHN

I first intended the Copper John to be fished under a high-floating Hopper with a more realistic pattern, the dropper, attached to the bend of the Copper John, to correlate with recent insect activity. I call this combination of flies Hopper-Copper-Dropper, or HCD for short. When HCD fishing, I use a 9-foot, 4-weight, fast-action rod and a floating line. Many people think that a 4-weight is not a heavy enough rod to effectively cast three flies, one of which is a large foam grasshopper imitation, but I have found that a good leader design can really help turn over this rig. When fishing the HCD, the Copper John is always first in line under the floating fly. I use a tapered 7½-foot 3X regular mono leader with a heavy butt section to the B/C Hopper, 2 to 4 feet (length varies with water depth) of 4X fluorocarbon to

the Copper John, and about 12 inches of 5X fluorocarbon tippet to the dropper. This progression helps turn over the flies and reduce tangles.

At first I only fished the Copper John under a floating fly, but I caught so many fish on the Copper John, I began to use it when nymphing. When nymph-fishing, I also use a 9-foot 4-weight with a 9-foot leader tapered to 3X. I add 3X, 4X, or 5X fluorocarbon as tippet, depending on the size of the fish I may encounter. I use a five-turn standard clinch knot for all my connections to hook eyes and hook bends. An improved clinch knot does not seat well with fluorocarbon. Copper Johns can be the first, second, and third flies or the first and second fly. It is usually the first fly, with nymphs imitating whatever aquatic insect activity is prevalent tied off the bend of the Copper John.

Often the Copper John provides enough weight, especially in sizes 12 and 14, that you do not have to use any split shot, but if you are fishing heavy, deep water you may have to add some. I know guides that hardly ever use split shot when fishing a Copper John because

The Copper John has worked well for me everywhere I've fished. This large Great Lakes brown was fooled by a #14 red Copper. LANDON MAYER

split shot tends to hinge the cast and foul the leader if you don't cast properly.

Stillwater Fishing

The Copper John is a lethal stillwater pattern fished either under an indicator or retrieved. I generally fish red, chartreuse, or the zebra in still waters. For pressured fish, an effective approach is to use three flies under an indicator, where legal. The first fly is a Copper John in either red or chartreuse with a nymph or pupa of the prevailing insect activity tied off the bend. If you see adult damselflies, for example, a damselfly nymph would be a logical choice to tie off the bend of the Copper. A midge larva is often a good choice for the third fly. I get many takes just letting it remain stationary. Sometimes I retrieve the fly with a hand twist, let it sit, and hand twist it again until it is back to the boat. When you pick the flies up to recast, don't just rip the flies out of the lake. Slowly lift the flies to the surface. Sometimes a fish will take the flies as they are being raised.

One of the best stillwater fishermen in the country, Doug Ouellette of Calvada Fly Fishing in Reno,

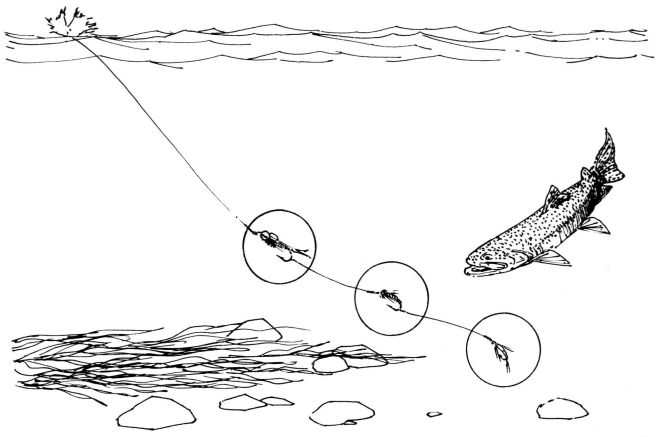

I frequently use a high floating B/C Hopper to suspend my nymphs, but you can also use a large poly strike indicator or another type of float. Copper Johns can be the first, second, and third flies or the first and second fly. I usually fish a Copper John as the first fly and then tie nymphs off the bend of the Copper John to imitate the prevailing insects.

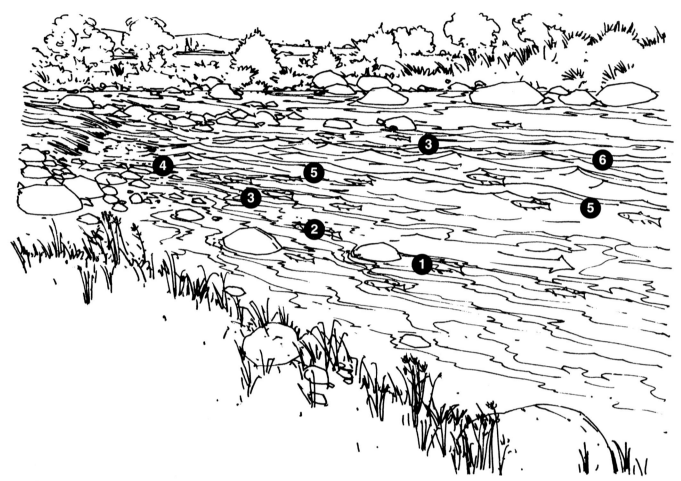

By adjusting the length of tippet between the buoyant dry fly and your nymphs, you can fish a wide range of water types—from pocket water (2) to deep runs (4, 5). Concentrate on current seams (3), the head of the run (4), behind rocks (1), and deeper riffles with moderate current speeds (6).

When fishing the Hopper-Dropper, cast upstream and follow the drift of the Hopper downstream with your rod tip. If necessary, retrieve extra slack with your line hand so that you can set the hook quickly when you detect a strike (or a fish hits your Hopper). I often keep the rod low and almost parallel to the water during the entire drift.

When setting the hook, don't lift your rod tip straight up. Instead, set the hook by striking horizontally, simultaneously stripping in slack with your line hand.

Nevada, sent me the following letter. Doug refers to his technique as Floater-No-Cater:

"The Copper John is an outstanding stillwater pattern. It has produced many large fish in famous western lakes, such as Pyramid, Nevada, Eagle, and Klamath lakes in Oregon. It is also a deadly pattern in our local reservoirs and private ponds. The Copper John can be fished alone or in tandem under an indicator with great results; however, I usually prefer to fish the Copper John with a floating line, a 14-foot fluorocarbon leader, and no indicator. Most of the time I'll use two Copper Johns, with the heavier fly back on the point and a smaller one on the dropper. One of the most effective techniques is as follows: after the cast, allow the Copper John to drop by using the countdown method. As the fly is sinking, watch the line for any unusual movement. Trout love to grab on the drop. Once the Copper John has settled, begin a very quick, very short erratic retrieve. These quick pops or 'binks' should only be ¼ to 2 inches long, with a retrieve pattern like this: bink, bink, bink, pause 2–4 seconds, bink, bink, pause 2–4 seconds, bink,

bink, bink, pause. Continue repeating this cadence until you have finished your retrieve. Because the Copper John is moving in this quick, erratic manner the fish will usually grab it hard. I believe this retrieve imitates the snapping, wiggling motion of an ascending midge."

Doug's method of fishing still waters was brand new to me. Since receiving Doug's letter, I've tried this technique on local lakes, and it is an effective approach. Because trout take the fly so hard, I use 3X fluorocarbon for both the red and the chartreuse Copper Johns.

Other Species

The Copper John isn't only effective on trout. It works well for steelhead and warmwater species such as bass, carp, and panfish. I have read reports and heard firsthand that the Copper John is a good steelhead pattern in some of the California and Oregon rivers and in the Great Lakes steelhead rivers. Another good friend, Trapper Rudd, owner of Cutthroat Anglers in Silverthorne, Colorado, even caught a bonefish on a Copper John that I tied for him on a saltwater hook with lead dumbbell eyes instead of a bead.

The Copper John is also a lethal panfish pattern. I often fish it under a Hopper and just let it sit or retrieve it in slowly with a hand twist. I suspend the Copper under a size 6 B/C Hopper in case the panfish have a hankering for surface flies. Sometimes I fish it without a Hopper and slowly retrieve it in. While fishing for panfish with these two techniques I have inadvertently hooked many bass.

I have caught both common and grass carp on the Copper John. When fishing for common carp I usually only cast to carp feeding on the bottom. When carp are feeding you can see puffs of silt on the bottom, and if the water is shallow enough, their tails may stick out of the water. This behavior is called tailing. You have to get the fly right in their faces, do a slow hand twist, and if you feel tension, set the hook. Grass carp are very difficult to catch on a fly. They are placed in ponds to help control vegetation, which they eat. They cruise around ponds near the surface, usually in schools, and spook easily. I have had some success throwing a size 10 B/C Hopper with a size 16 red or chartreuse about a foot below the Hopper. Cast well ahead of the school and just let your flies sit motionless. I have caught grass carp on both flies. The other day I arrived at a pond as a guy was landing a 25-pound common carp that he caught on a size 14 red Copper John. Both common carp and grass carp are very strong and in shallow water can go on some impressive runs.

The Copper John in various colors and sizes works for everything from panfish to Great Lakes steelhead (above). JAY NICHOLS

Landon Mayer (above) caught this 30-inch, 11-pound brown trout on a sunny afternoon on October 12, 2004, with a size 20 Copper John. LANDON MAYER

Variations of the original evolved over time. First, I added a tungsten bead, then rubber legs, and finally created the Jumbo John, an oversize Copper John tied with a large hen collar and bright bead for steelhead. All these patterns are tied on a curved hook, which gives them a different look. There are no set guidelines to determine which style to use. Some of the variables to consider are the type of water you are fishing, the size of the fish, and your own intuition.

"Some of the most memorable and successful days I have fished on many waters have been the result of fishing the Copper John. The fly is a unique creation that can be fished effectively in various water situations, large or small, all over the United States and the world. It can be a close imitation of multiple aquatic food sources, as well as a great attractor fly for triggering strikes. My fondest memory of fishing the Copper John was the sunny afternoon of October 12, 2004, when I landed a 30-inch, 11-pound brown on a size 20 Copper John. This trout ended up as the state record on 4-pound-test. This is one of the most rewarding trout I have ever landed, not only because of its size, but because of the friendship with John that followed. You can't go wrong with a Copper John."

—LANDON MAYER, guide and author,
Colorado Springs, Colorado

ORIGINAL COPPER JOHN

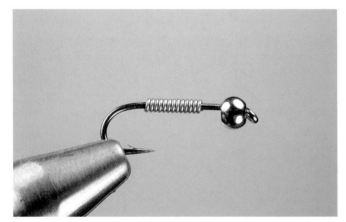

1. Place the bead on the hook by inserting the hook point into the smaller hole on the front of the bead. Slide the bead up to the hook eye. Insert the hook into the vise. Wrap thirteen turns of lead wire onto the hook shank from the back of the hook to the front.

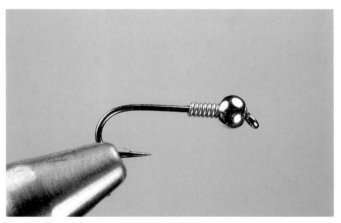

2. Break off both ends of the lead with your thumbnail. Shove the lead wraps up into the back of the bead, countersinking the wraps into the recess.

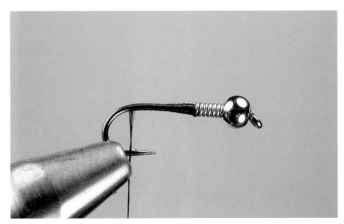

3. Start the tying thread at the back edge of the lead wraps. Build a smooth taper from the bare hook shank up to the lead wire and continue with a smooth thread base back to the bend of the hook. Leave the tying thread hanging at the bend.

HOOK SIZE	BEAD
12	$^1/_8$ inch
14–16	$^7/_{64}$ inch
18	$^3/_{32}$ inch

HOOK SIZE	LEAD WIRE
12	.020 inch
14–16	.015 inch
18	.010 inch
20–22	no lead

HOOK SIZE	ULTRA WIRE
12	medium
14–16	Brassie
18–22	small

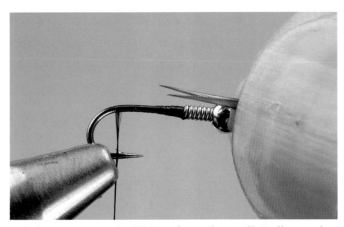

4. Select two matched biots from the quill. Pull two that are right next to each other to assure that they are the same width and length. Place the biots back to back so they curve away from each other, and even their tips. Measure the biots against the hook shank so they are equal to one-half a shank length long.

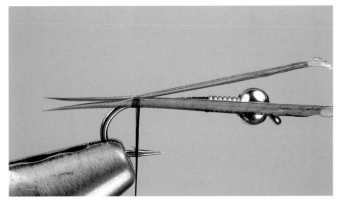

6. Wrap two turns of thread over the biots to hold them in place on the near side of the hook. If you tie them in at a slight angle, thread torque pulls them onto the correct position. Pull the tying thread down to tighten the loops of thread and pull the biots on top of the hook shank.

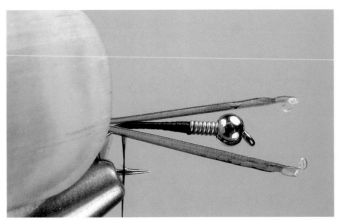

5. Place the opposed biots at the hook bend with one on each side of the hook shank. Turn them so they are slightly off-center toward the near side of the hook.

7. Wrap forward over the butt ends of the biots to just in front of the hook point.

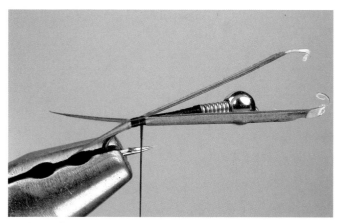

8. Properly tied-in biot tails.

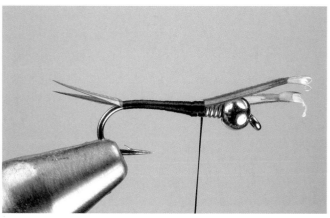

9. Continue wrapping forward over the butt ends of the biots up to and onto the lead wraps. The butt ends will help build the taper to the lead wraps.

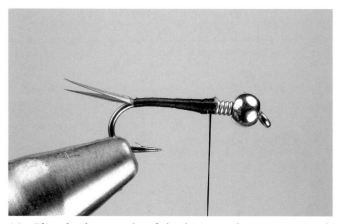

10. Clip the butt ends of the biots and wrap a smooth thread base from the base of the tail to the three-quarter point on the shank. The thread base should be as smooth as possible and have an even taper from front to back.

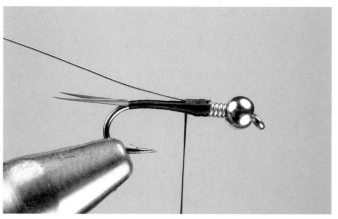

11. Cut a length of copper wire about 6 or 8 inches long and tie it in at the front of the thread underbody on top of the hook.

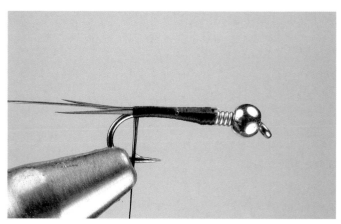

12. Wrap back over the copper wire to the base of the tails. Make several tight turns of thread coming forward from the bend to secure the wire. Keep these thread wraps as smooth as possible.

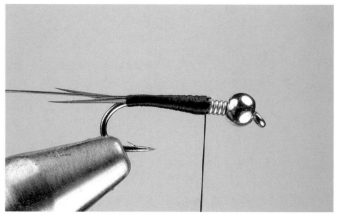

13. Continue forward with the thread to the front end of the abdomen.

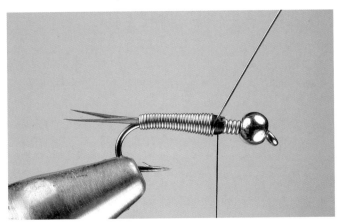

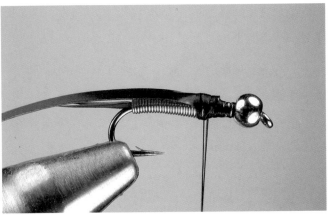

14. Begin wrapping the wire forward from the hook bend in tight, concentric turns. Tilting the wire back slightly as you wrap will allow the next wrap to roll off the edge of the previous wrap, butting the turns together. Continue wrapping the copper wire forward to the end of the thread underbody. Tie the wire off at the front edge of the underbody with two tight turns of thread. Clip the excess wire with a pair of nail clippers, or twist the remaining end around in a circle until it breaks off. Cover the stub end with a few turns of tying thread.

16. Cut a strip of Thin Skin slightly narrower than the width of the hook gap. Leave the Thin Skin on the paper backing while you cut the strip. If you remove the whole sheet it will roll up into an unusable ball. After you cut the strip to the correct width, peel the Thin Skin strip from the paper backing.

Tie the Thin Skin strip in on top of the hook shank at the front of the abdomen and wrap back over it to the 70 percent point on the hook shank. Tie the Thin Skin in with the shiny side (the side that was adhered to the paper backing) facing up.

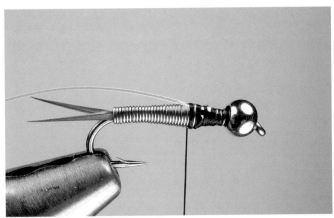

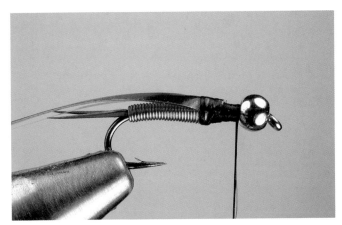

15. Cover the lead wraps between the copper wire abdomen and the back of the bead with a thin layer of thread. Only use enough thread to eliminate the spaces between the lead wire. Tie in a single strand of pearl Flashabou directly on top of the hook and make certain that it is centered on the hook. Wrap back over the Flashabou and the front end of the copper abdomen so it is tied in back to the point shown.

17. Wrap the thread forward to a point just behind the bead.

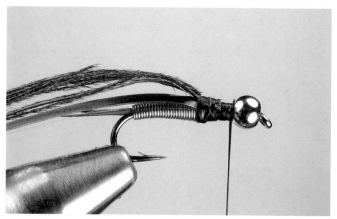

18. Select five or six bushy peacock herls and trim their tips evenly. Tie the peacock in by its tips just behind the bead and wrap back over them to the base of the Thin Skin wing case. Return the thread to the back edge of the bead.

19. Wrap the peacock herls forward in tight, concentric, non-overlapping turns to the back of the bead and tie them off with a couple tight turns of thread.

20. Clip the excess peacock flush.

21. Pull a small clump of fibers from the side of a hen-back feather to align the tips. Peel the clump from the stem of the feather.

22. Lay the clump of hen fibers along the far side of the hook shank with the tips extending back to the hook point. Press the fibers against the hook with your index finger.

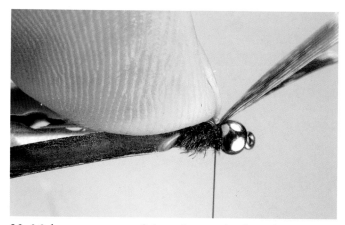

23. Make two turns of thread over the hen fibers right behind the bead.

24. Prepare and strip another like-sized clump of fibers from the hen feather. Tie this clump in along the near side of the hook.

25. Trim the butt ends from both clumps.

26. Pull the Thin Skin forward over the top of the peacock thorax and tie it down right behind the bead.

27. Pull the Flashabou over the top of the Thin Skin, making sure it runs down the center of the wing case. Tie the Flashabou down right behind the bead.

28. Close-up.

29. Clip the butt ends of the Flashabou and the Thin Skin as close to the bead as you can. Build a smooth thread head and whip-finish the thread.

30. Mix a small batch of epoxy and coat the wing case from front to back and side to side. It helps to run the epoxy up onto the back edge of the bead and down onto the wire at the back of the wing case.

31. Top view.

PATTERN VARIATIONS

COPPER JOHN
(Chartreuse)

Hook:	Size 10–18 Tiemco 5262
Bead:	Gold
Weight:	Lead wire
Thread:	Black 70-denier Ultra Thread
Tail:	Black goose biots
Abdomen:	Chartreuse Ultra Wire
Wing case:	Black Thin Skin and pearl Flashabou covered with epoxy
Thorax:	Peacock herl
Legs:	Black hen back

COPPER JOHN
(Black)

Hook:	Size 10–18 Tiemco 5262
Bead:	Gold
Weight:	Lead wire
Thread:	Black 70-denier Ultra Thread
Tail:	Black goose biots
Abdomen:	Black Ultra Wire
Wing case:	Black Thin Skin and pearl Flashabou covered with epoxy
Thorax:	Peacock herl
Legs:	Black hen back

COPPER JOHN
(Blue)

Hook:	Size 10–18 Tiemco 5262
Bead:	Gold
Weight:	Lead wire
Thread:	Black 70-denier Ultra Thread
Tail:	Black goose biots
Abdomen:	Blue Ultra Wire
Wing case:	Black Thin Skin and pearl Flashabou covered with epoxy
Thorax:	Peacock herl
Legs:	Black hen back

COPPER JOHN
(Zebra)

Hook:	Size 10–18 Tiemco 5262
Bead:	Silver
Weight:	Lead wire
Thread:	Black 70-denier Ultra Thread
Tail:	Black goose biots
Abdomen:	Black and silver Ultra Wire
Wing case:	Black Thin Skin and pearl Flashabou covered with epoxy
Thorax:	Peacock herl
Legs:	Black hen back

COPPER JOHN
(Wine)

Hook:	Size 10–18 Tiemco 5262
Bead:	Gold
Weight:	Lead wire
Thread:	Black 70-denier Ultra Thread
Tail:	White goose biots
Abdomen:	Wine Ultra Wire
Wing case:	Black Thin Skin and pearl Flashabou covered with epoxy
Thorax:	Peacock herl
Legs:	Mottled brown hen back

COPPER JOHN
(Red)

Hook:	Size 10–18 Tiemco 5262
Bead:	Gold
Weight:	Lead wire
Thread:	Black 70-denier Ultra Thread
Tail:	Brown goose biots
Abdomen:	Red Ultra Wire
Wing case:	Black Thin Skin and pearl Flashabou covered with epoxy
Thorax:	Peacock herl
Legs:	Mottled brown hen back

COPPER JOHN
(Silver)

Hook:	Size 10–18 Tiemco 5262
Bead:	Black
Weight:	Lead wire
Thread:	Black 70-denier Ultra Thread
Tail:	Black goose biots
Abdomen:	Silver Ultra Wire
Wing case:	Black Thin Skin and pearl Flashabou covered with epoxy
Thorax:	Peacock herl
Legs:	Black hen back

COPPER JOHN
(Pink)

Hook:	Size 10–18 Tiemco 5262
Bead:	Black
Weight:	Lead wire
Thread:	Black 70-denier Ultra Thread
Tail:	Black goose biots
Abdomen:	Hot pink Ultra Wire
Wing case:	Black Thin Skin and pearl Flashabou covered with epoxy
Thorax:	Peacock herl
Legs:	Black hen back

COPPER JOHN
(Copper Brown)

Hook:	Size 10–18 Tiemco 5262
Bead:	Copper
Weight:	Lead wire
Thread:	Black 70-denier Ultra Thread
Tail:	Brown goose biots
Abdomen:	Copper brown Ultra Wire
Wing case:	Black Thin Skin and pearl Flashabou covered with epoxy
Thorax:	Peacock herl
Legs:	Mottled brown hen back

COPPER JOHN
(Green)

Hook:	Size 10–18 Tiemco 5262
Bead:	Copper
Weight:	Lead wire
Thread:	Black 70-denier Ultra Thread
Tail:	Black goose biots
Abdomen:	Green Ultra Wire
Wing case:	Black Thin Skin and pearl Flashabou covered with epoxy
Thorax:	Peacock herl
Legs:	Black hen back

CHAPTER 2

Tungsten Bead Copper John

Because it can be difficult to hook and hold large fish with small hooks, I decided to build a version of my Copper John on a small hook that had excellent hook-setting and fish-holding qualities. The Tungsten Bead Copper John is tied in sizes 16 through 20 on the Tiemco 2488, which is a short-shank curved hook with a 3X wide gap. The extra-wide hook gap on this model provides terrific hooking capabilities for a small fly. A size 16 Tiemco 2488 is roughly equal to a size 20 standard length shank hook, but it has the gap of a standard size 12.

Tied on a curved hook, this fly might look like a nymph partially curled up as it drifts in the current. The tungsten bead helps this small pattern sink quickly. Like the original Copper, this fly can be tied in a wide range of colors, but red, copper, and chartreuse are mainstays in my box.

CHARLIE CRAVEN

TUNGSTEN BEAD COPPER JOHN
(Copper)

Hook:	Size 16–20 Tiemco 2488 or 2488H
Bead:	Gold tungsten
Thread:	Black 8/0 Uni-Thread
Tail:	Black hackle fibers
Abdomen:	Copper Ultra Wire (small)
Wing case:	Brown Thin Skin and holographic silver Flashabou coated with epoxy
Thorax:	Bronze Arizona synthetic peacock dubbing
Legs:	Butt ends of tail fibers

Tungsten Bead Copper Johns are versions of the original Copper John tied on smaller hooks. My favorite colors are copper, red, and chartreuse. CHARLIE CRAVEN

I often tie the Tungsten Bead Copper John on a curved shank hook, but you can also tie them on straight-eye, straight-shank hooks in a wide variety of colors. CHARLIE CRAVEN

This rainbow fell for a size 20 red Tungsten Copper John trailed behind a size 14 Copper John. LANDON MAYER

TUNGSTEN BEAD COPPER JOHN

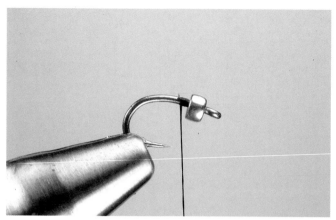

1. Slide the bead onto the hook and push it up to the eye of the hook. Insert the hook into the vise. Start the tying thread immediately behind the bead.

2. Tie in about a dozen black hackle fibers right behind the bead. Leave some length sticking up behind the bead, as these fibers will become the legs on the finished fly.

3. Wrap back over the tips of the hackle fibers about halfway down the bend of the hook.

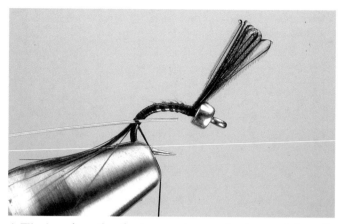

4. Tie in a length of wire starting at the base of the tail.

5. Wrap forward over the wire to the midpoint of the hook.

6. Wrap the wire forward in tight concentric turns to the midpoint. Tie off the wire and clip the excess.

7. Tie in a single strand of silver holographic Flashabou on top of the wire. Wrap back over the flash to the hook point.

8. Tie in a strip of black Thin Skin that is about half as wide as the hook gap. Wrap back over the Thin Skin to the hook point.

9. Dub the thread and form a round thorax with the dubbing. Leave just a bit of space right behind the bead.

10. Divide the butt ends of the hackle fibers into two equal bunches. Pull these bunches to the sides of the hook.

11. Hold the hackle fiber bunches back along the body of the fly and make a turn or two of dubbing between the hackle fibers and the bead. The dubbing will force the legs back along the sides of the fly.

12. Pull the Thin Skin over the top of the thorax and tie it down behind the bead.

13. Pull the Flashabou over the top of the Thin Skin and tie it down behind the bead as well. Be sure the flash is centered on the wing case.

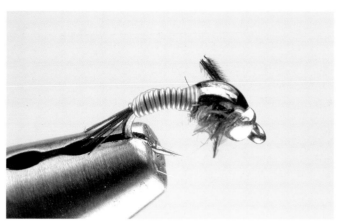

15. Coat the wing case with epoxy.

14. Clip the butt ends of the flash and Thin Skin, make a few turns of thread to cover the stubs, and whip-finish.

PATTERN VARIATIONS

CHARLIE CRAVEN

CHARLIE CRAVEN

TUNGSTEN BEAD COPPER JOHN
(Red)

Hook:	Size 16–20 Tiemco 2488 or 2488H
Bead:	Gold tungsten
Thread:	Black 8/0 Uni-Thread
Tail:	Brown hackle fibers
Abdomen:	Red Ultra Wire (small)
Wing case:	Black Thin Skin and holographic silver Flashabou coated with epoxy
Thorax:	Bronze Arizona synthetic peacock dubbing
Legs:	Butt ends of tail fibers

TUNGSTEN BEAD COPPER JOHN
(Chartreuse)

Hook:	Size 16–20 Tiemco 2488 or 2488H
Bead:	Gold tungsten
Thread:	Black 8/0 Uni-Thread
Tail:	Black hackle fibers
Abdomen:	Chartreuse Ultra Wire (small)
Wing case:	Black Thin Skin and holographic silver Flashabou coated with epoxy
Thorax:	Bronze Arizona synthetic peacock dubbing
Legs:	Butt ends of tail fibers

CHAPTER 3

Rubber Leg Copper John

This version of the Copper John is tied on the Tiemco 2499SP-BL (special point, barbless), but I added rubber legs and two colors of copper wire. I am not sure if the two-tone abdomen works better than one color of wire, but it looks good and is effective. I started experimenting with wrapping two colors of wire shortly after Wapsi introduced Ultra Wire. At first I wrapped a single color and ribbed that color with another color. Then I discovered I could wrap both pieces of wire at the same time as long as I maintained tension on the two strands of wire. I experimented with numerous color combinations and finally settled on four: black and olive with a gold bead, copper and copper brown with a copper bead, black and silver (zebra) with a black bead, and blue and red with a gold bead. Since the original four colors, I have added several more variations. All of the patterns have black rubber legs.

The new pattern proved to be effective for trout that were looking for something a little different than the original version of the Copper John. There is just something about rubber legs that trout find attractive. Maybe they add a little extra animation to the pattern.

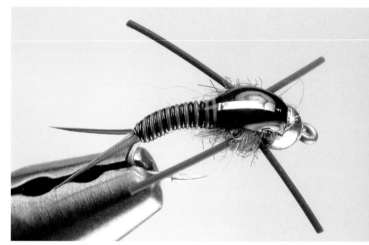

CHARLIE CRAVEN

RUBBER LEG COPPER JOHN
(Olive and Black)

Hook:	Size 10–18 Tiemco 2499SP-BL
Bead:	Gold tungsten
Weight:	Lead wire (see chart)
Thread:	Black 70-denier Ultra Thread
Tail:	Brown goose biots
Abdomen:	Olive and black Ultra Wire (Brassie)
Wing case:	Black Thin Skin and holographic silver Flashabou coated with epoxy
Thorax:	Bronze Arizona synthetic peacock dubbing
Legs:	Round black rubber legs (extra small)

Large trout find undulating rubber legs irresistible. I caught this fish on a small fly trailed behind a Rubber Leg Copper John, but I'm sure it was the large rubber legs moving in the current that first caught the fish's attention. LANDON MAYER

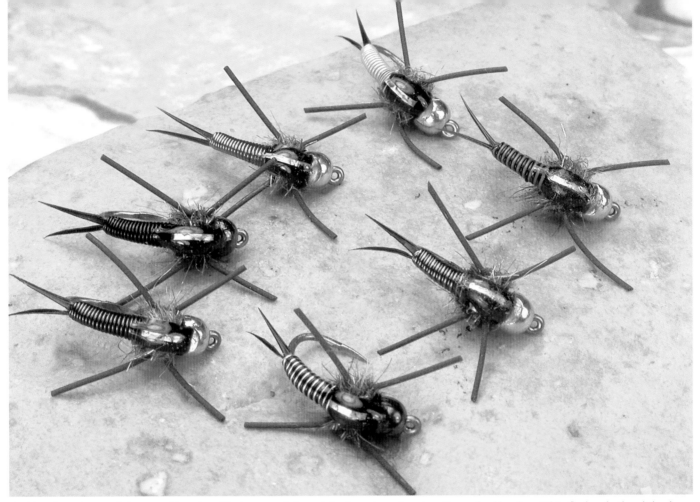

Rubber Leg Copper Johns combine the effectiveness of the original version plus the allure of rubber legs. This fly has both solid colors of wire and two colors of wire wrapped together for a variegated effect. Chartreuse, red, black, green (left row), and olive/black, blue/red, and zebra colors shown above. CHARLIE CRAVEN

RUBBER LEG COPPER JOHN

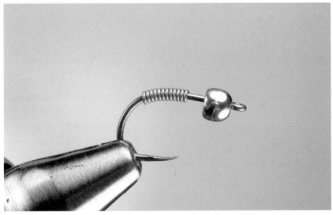

1. Place the bead on the hook and slide it up to the eye. Insert the hook into the vise. Make thirteen wraps of .015-inch-diameter lead wire around the shank behind the bend and break off the loose ends.

HOOK SIZE	BEAD
10	3.3 mm
12	2.8 mm
14	2.8 mm
16	2.3 mm
18	2.0 mm

HOOK SIZE	LEAD WIRE
10–12	.020 inch
14–16	.015 inch
18	.010 inch

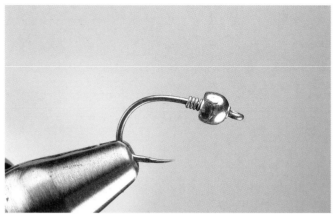

2. Shove the lead wraps up into the bead, forcing them all the way to the front of the hook. This will center the bead on the shank and add additional weight to the fly.

3. Start the tying thread behind the lead wire and build a smooth taper up onto the lead wrap. Continue the thread base up to the back of the bead and all the way back about halfway down the bend of the hook.

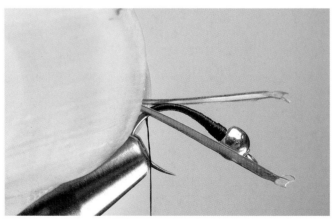

4. Reposition the hook in the vise so the bend is more exposed. Select two brown goose biots and oppose their curves. Measure the biots so they are about one-half the shank length long. Place the tie-in point on the biots above the last thread wrap at the back of the hook with each biot on opposite sides of the shank. Tilt the biots slightly toward you, so they are off-center to the near side of the hook.

5. Make two wraps of thread over the biots. Let the thread torque turn the biots to top dead center on the hook shank as you tighten the thread. Wrap forward over the butt ends of the biots to lock them in place. The tails should be nicely split and square on top of the hook shank.

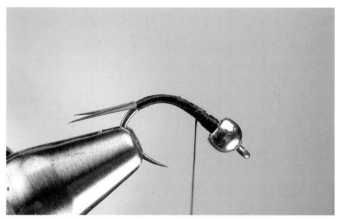

6. Wrap forward over the butt ends of the biots up to just behind the bead. Take care to keep a smooth thread base as you go. Clip the excess biot flush with the shank.

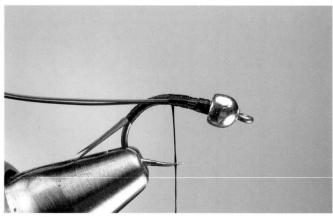

7. Tie in one strand of olive wire and one strand of black wire. Keep the ends of the wire even and tie them in as one unit.

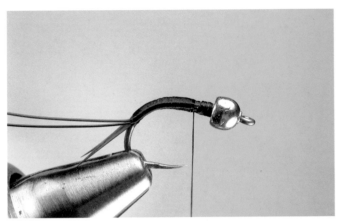

8. Wrap back over the wires to the base of the tails. Return the thread to just in front of the hook point. Be sure to keep the thread underbody smooth and slightly tapered at the front as you go. Pull both strands of wire straight out the back of the hook to align them.

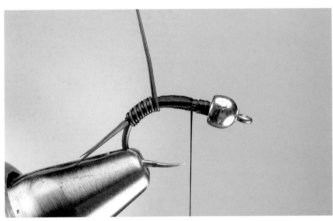

9. Wrap both strands of wire at the same time forward from the base of the tail as one unit. Do not let the wires twist as you wrap; they should lie one next to the other as shown here.

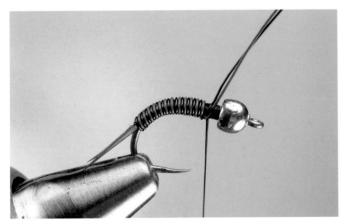

10. Wrap the wires forward to just in front of the hook point and tie them off.

11. Break off the excess wire and wrap the thread slightly back over the front edge of the wire abdomen. The thread should be hanging even with the point on the hook.

12. Tie in a single strand of holographic silver Flashabou directly atop the hook shank and wrap back over it to the hook point. Make certain the flash is centered on top of the hook.

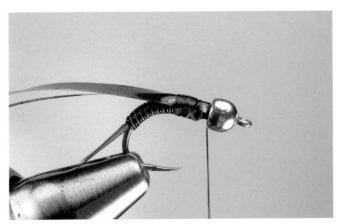

13. Tie in a strip of black Thin Skin and wrap back over it to the same point that the flash is tied in.

14. Dub the thorax to full size with the bronze peacock dubbing. End with the thread hanging in the center of the dubbing. Make a couple wraps of thread right in the middle of the dubbed thorax.

15. Tie in one strand of extra-small black rubber leg material on the near side of the hook in the center of the thorax dubbing. Use only two wraps to secure this strand.

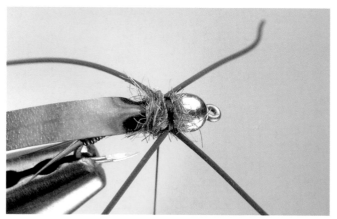

16. Tie in another strand of rubber along the far side of the thorax.

17. Dub a little more fur onto the thread and use it to cover the tie-down of the rubber legs.

18. Advance the dubbed thread forward to the back of the bead.

19. Pull the black Thin Skin over the top of the thorax and tie it down tightly behind the bead. Do not clip the Thin Skin yet.

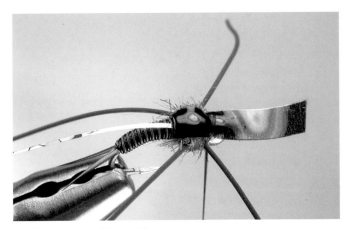

20. Top view of Thin Skin wing case.

23. Legs should look like this.

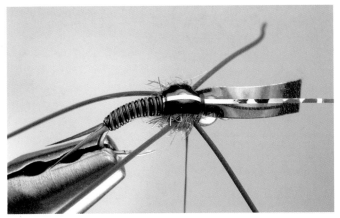

21. Pull the Flashabou forward over the top of the wing case, taking care to keep it centered across the top of the hook, and tie it down behind the bead as well.

24. Trim the rubber legs so the back legs reach the end of the wire body and the front legs are just slightly shorter.

22. Clip the stub ends of both the Thin Skin and the flash as close to the bead as you can. Build a smooth thread head behind the bead to cover the stubs and wrap slightly over the front rubber legs.

25. Place a drop of epoxy over the top of the thorax, making sure to completely coat the wing case from side to side and front to back. The epoxy will stick to the fly much better if you extend the epoxy coating onto the last couple turns of wire as well as onto the back edge of the bead. Place the fly in a block of foam to dry.

PATTERN VARIATIONS

RUBBER LEG COPPER JOHN
(Red and Blue)

Hook:	Size 10–18 Tiemco 2499SP-BL
Bead:	Gold tungsten
Weight:	Lead wire
Thread:	Black 70-denier Ultra Thread
Tail:	Black goose biots
Abdomen:	Red and blue Ultra Wire (Brassie)
Wing case:	Black Thin Skin and holographic silver Flashabou coated with epoxy
Thorax:	Bronze Arizona synthetic peacock dubbing
Legs:	Round black rubber legs (extra small)

RUBBER LEG COPPER JOHN
(Zebra)

Hook:	Size 10–18 Tiemco 2499SP-BL
Bead:	Black tungsten
Weight:	Lead wire
Thread:	Black 70-denier Ultra Thread
Tail:	Black goose biots
Abdomen:	Silver and black Ultra Wire
Wing case:	Black Thin Skin and holographic silver Flashabou
Thorax:	Natural Arizona synthetic peacock dubbing
Legs:	Round black rubber legs (extra small)

RUBBER LEG COPPER JOHN
(Copper/Copper Brown)

Hook:	Size 10–18 Tiemco 2499SP-BL
Bead:	Copper tungsten
Weight:	Lead wire
Thread:	Black 70-denier Ultra Thread
Tail:	Brown goose biots
Abdomen:	Copper and copper brown Ultra Wire (Brassie)
Wing case:	Black Thin Skin and holographic silver Flashabou coated with epoxy
Thorax:	Bronze Arizona synthetic peacock dubbing
Legs:	Round black rubber legs (extra small)

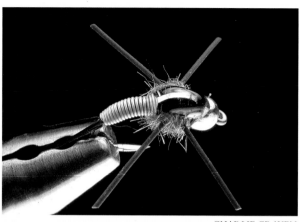

CHARLIE CRAVEN

RUBBER LEG COPPER JOHN
(Chartreuse)

Hook:	Size 10–18 Tiemco 2499SP-BL
Bead:	Gold tungsten
Weight:	Lead wire
Thread:	Black 70-denier Ultra Thread
Tail:	Black goose biots
Abdomen:	Chartreuse Ultra Wire (Brassie)
Wing case:	Black Thin Skin and holographic silver Flashabou coated with epoxy
Thorax:	Bronze Arizona synthetic peacock dubbing
Legs:	Round black rubber legs (extra small)

RUBBER LEG COPPER JOHN
(Black)

Hook:	Size 10–18 Tiemco 2499SP-BL
Bead:	Black tungsten
Weight:	Lead wire
Thread:	Black 70-denier Ultra Thread
Tail:	Black goose biots
Abdomen:	Black Ultra Wire (Brassie)
Wing case:	Black Thin Skin and holographic silver Flashabou coated with epoxy
Thorax:	Bronze Arizona synthetic peacock dubbing
Legs:	Round black rubber legs (extra small)

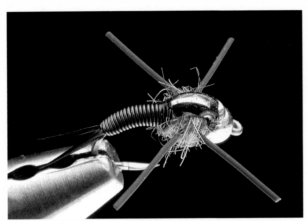

CHARLIE CRAVEN

RUBBER LEG COPPER JOHN
(Green)

Hook:	Size 10–18 Tiemco 2499SP-BL
Bead:	Gold tungsten
Weight:	Lead wire
Thread:	Black 70-denier Ultra Thread
Tail:	Black goose biots
Abdomen:	Green Ultra Wire (Brassie)
Wing case:	Black Thin Skin and holographic silver Flashabou coated with epoxy
Thorax:	Bronze Arizona synthetic peacock dubbing
Legs:	Round black rubber legs (extra small)

CHARLIE CRAVEN

RUBBER LEG COPPER JOHN
(Red)

Hook:	Size 10–18 Tiemco 2499SP-BL
Bead:	Gold tungsten
Weight:	Lead wire
Thread:	Black 70-denier Ultra Thread
Tail:	Brown goose biots
Abdomen:	Red Ultra Wire (Brassie)
Wing case:	Black Thin Skin and holographic silver Flashabou coated with epoxy
Thorax:	Bronze Arizona synthetic peacock dubbing
Legs:	Round black rubber legs (extra small)

CHAPTER 4

Jumbo John

The Jumbo John completes the Copper John series. Steelhead fishermen who had success with the original Copper John requested a pattern with popular steelhead-fly features such as a hen collar and bright fluorescent bead. The Jumbo John is tied on the Tiemco 2499SP-BL in sizes 6 and 8. The large hook accommodates lots of lead wire and the large bead helps this fly sink like an anchor, essential in fast flows when steelhead are holding on the bottom and won't move far to take a fly. The colors are black (black wire with a salmon colored bead), golden stone (black and ginger wire with a gold bead), and copper (copper and copper/brown wire with an orange bead). All patterns have a hen back collar.

Not only is this pattern great for dead-drifting nymphs to steelhead, but it is also a good pattern for trout wherever stoneflies are found, especially the golden stone color. The Jumbo John can be very effective trailed behind a streamer.

"Having known John for many years, I often get a sneak peek at his new flies, fly developments, and have, on occasions, been the first on the block to test his new patterns. Such was the case on a trip to

CHARLIE CRAVEN

JUMBO JOHN
(Copper/Copper Brown)

Hook:	Size 6–10 Tiemco 2499SP-BL
Bead:	Hot orange brass bead (³⁄₁₆ inch)
Weight:	.020-inch-diameter lead wire
Thread:	Black 70- and 140-denier Ultra Thread
Tail:	Brown goose biots
Abdomen:	Copper and copper brown Ultra Wire (medium)
Wing case:	Brown Thin Skin and pearl saltwater Flashabou covered with epoxy
Thorax:	Bronze Arizona synthetic peacock dubbing
Legs:	Hot orange round rubber legs (medium)
Collar:	Mottled brown hen saddle

The Jumbo John is designed for large trout and steelhead (both West Coast and Great Lakes). I tie the pattern in all black, copper/copper brown, and ginger/black. CHARLIE CRAVEN

Tied in different sizes, the Jumbo John works well for Great Lakes steelhead (above). The bright bead resembles an egg. JAY NICHOLS

Tierra del Fuego a few years back, when John personally tied some of his prototype Jumbo Johns for me to use on the sea-run brown trout of the Rio Grande River. We both surmised that many Rio Grande browns had fallen prey to large nymph-type patterns often used for steelhead in the Great Lakes and western United States, and the Jumbo John seemed to fit this description perfectly. John tied a number of color combinations for me, but the one that caught my eye the most was an all-black fly with a salmon-colored bead head. This is the fly that hooked the fish that will forever leave its mark on my psyche.

"I had been swinging flies with a two-handed rod for much of the trip and having excellent success landing numerous fish over ten pounds, when I decided to fish a small heavy-water side channel that just looked too good to pass up. I put the two-handed aside and knotted up the black Jumbo John to a 9½-foot 8-weight rod and proceeded to deep-water nymph the run. On my third cast the line came tight, and initially I thought I was snagged on the bottom; after all, I was using a 300-grain sink

tip. Quickly I realized I was hooked to a big fish! My guide at Estancia Despedita, Ozzie, quickly came over to check out the action when a huge fish came to the surface and thrashed around. Many Spanish expletives flew from his mouth as we watched this behemoth of a fish struggle against the current and the bend of the rod. Ozzie went into instant guide mode, coaching me as we tried to figure out how to land the fish against the high bank. It was easily the biggest fish he had seen in his many years of guiding the river, figuring it above 40 pounds. 'A certain world record' he says to this day!

"Well, I wish I could tell you we won the battle and landed the fish. It was after numerous attempts to get it into the net, for it wouldn't fit, that the fish came unpinned and resumed the journey to its spawning habitat. The fish has become something of legend and lore at the lodge and I know that should I ever return to fish the Rio Grande River, I will certainly have more than a few Jumbo Johns in my box."

—MICHAEL WHITE, Blue Ribbon Sales,
Boulder, Colorado

This large Spinney Reservoir (Colorado) male brown hammered an all-black Jumbo John. LANDON MAYER

JUMBO JOHN

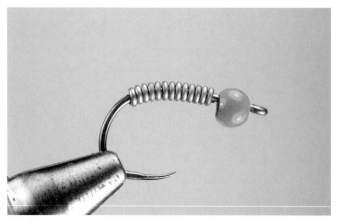

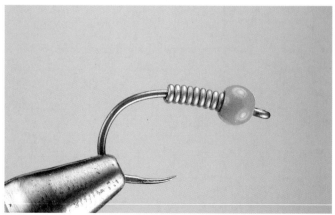

1. Place the bead on the hook and slide it up to the eye. Insert the hook into the vise. Make thirteen turns of lead wire around the shank and break off the ends.

2. Shove the lead wraps up into the bead as far as they will go.

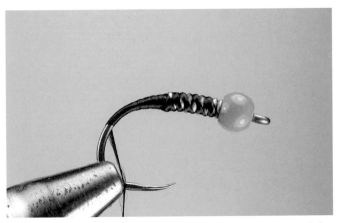

3. Start the 140-denier black thread at the base of the lead wraps and form a taper up to the lead. Continue building a thread base about one-third of the way down the hook bend.

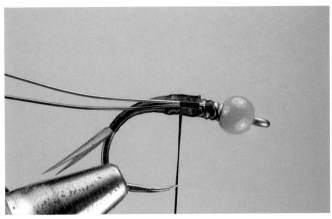

6. Cut two equal length strands of copper and copper brown wire and even their ends. Tie both strands of wire in along the near side of the hook about three eye lengths back from the hook eye.

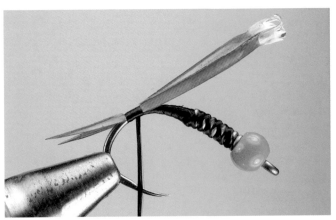

4. Oppose a pair of goose biots and tie them in at the end of the thread base.

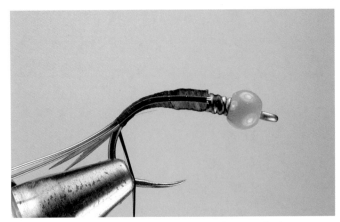

7. Wrap back over the two strands of wire all the way to the base of the tails with very tight wraps.

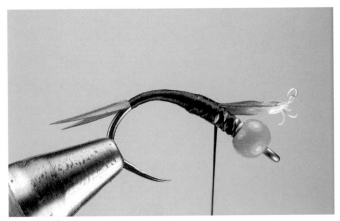

5. Wrap forward over the butt ends of the biot tails up to the lead wraps. The biots will help to smooth the underbody when you wrap over them tightly. Clip the excess butt ends up near the front of the hook.

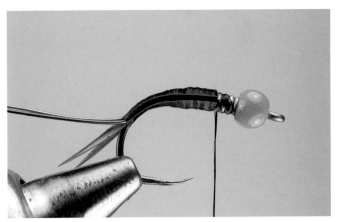

8. Move the thread back to the starting point, forming a smooth underbody as you go.

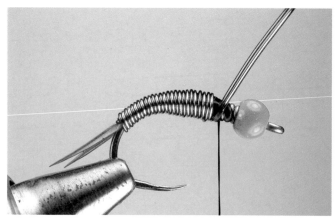

9. Wrap both strands of wire forward at the same time, forming the abdomen. Tie both strands off tightly at the front of the hook. Helicopter the ends of the wire to break them off.

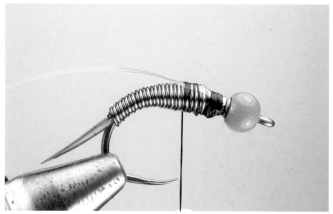

10. Tie in a single strand of pearl saltwater Flashabou on top of the hook at the front, and wrap back over it to just in front of the hook point.

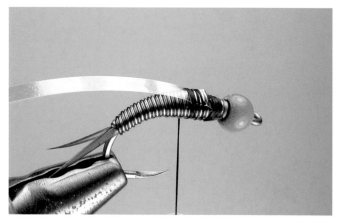

11. Detail of Flashabou tie-in.

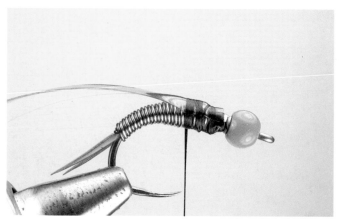

12. Cut a strip of Thin Skin about half as wide as the gap of the hook. Remove the paper backing and tie the Thin Skin in as you did with the flash and wrap back over it to just in front of the hook point.

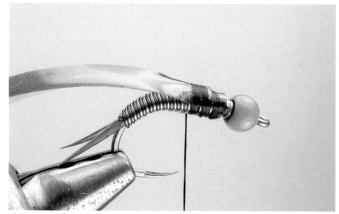

13. Detail of Thin Skin tie-in.

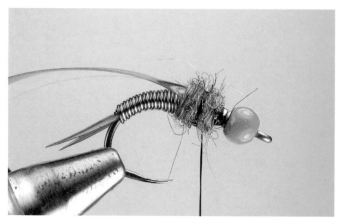

14. Twist some dubbing onto the thread and build a round thorax on the front third of the hook. Be sure to leave a bit of bare space between the dubbed thorax and the bead for the hackle collar. Make your dubbing wraps so that when you run out of dubbing, the thread is hanging in the middle of the thorax. Make two turns of bare thread right through the center of the dubbed thorax.

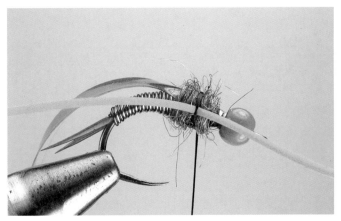

15. Tie in a strand of round rubber leg material along the near side of the hook at the center of the thorax.

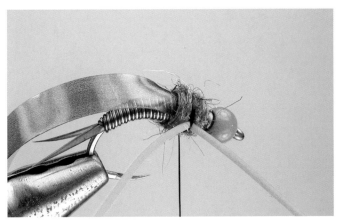

16. Detail of leg tie-in.

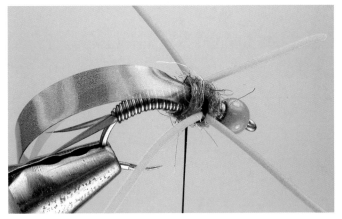

17. Tie in another strand of rubber leg material on the far side of the thorax.

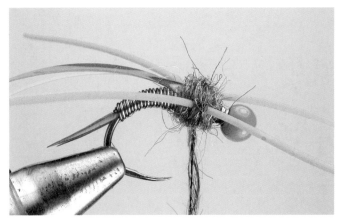

18. Tightly dub a tiny bit of dubbing on the thread and wrap it to cover the band of thread that holds the legs in place.

19. With the last turn of dubbing, move forward to just behind the bead so no bare thread shows in the thorax.

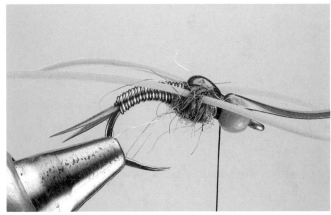

20. Pull the Thin Skin wing case tightly over the dubbed thorax and bind it down just behind the bead.

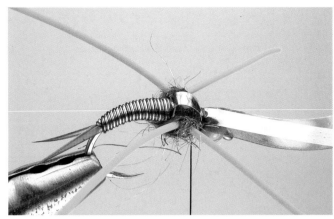

21. Pull the Flashabou over the top of the Thin Skin, taking care to keep it centered, and tie it down behind the bead as well.

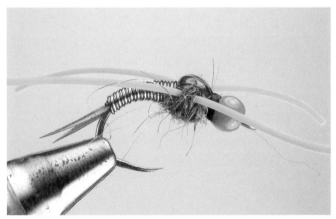

22. Clip the butt ends of the Flashabou and Thin Skin, make a few turns of thread to cover the stub ends, and whip-finish the 140-denier thread.

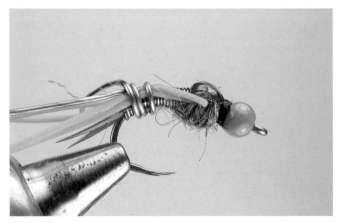

23. Wrap a scrap piece of lead wire around the shank and rubber legs to hold them out of the way while you epoxy the wing case.

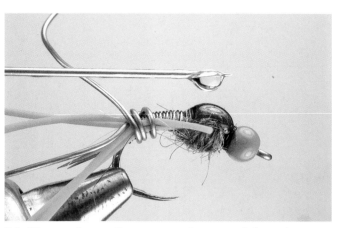

24. Place a drop of epoxy on the top of the wing case and smear it from side to side and front to back. Get some onto the last few turns of wire to improve durability, but be careful not to get any in the reserved space behind the bead. Set the fly aside while the epoxy dries completely. I usually stage tie several of these flies through this step and epoxy them all at once, then come back and do the collars once they have had time to cure.

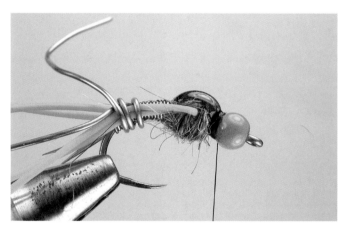

25. Start the 70-denier thread right behind the bead. Hot orange thread should be used here to match the bead, but I used black for photographic purposes.

26. Select and prepare a hen saddle feather that has barbs about as long as the hook shank. Tie the hen feather in by its butt end at the front of the wing case.

27. Lift the tip of the feather up and fold the hackle fibers back toward the bend of the hook.

28. Make a turn or two of the hen feather around the shank between the wing case and the bead. Tie off the hen feather and clip the remaining tip.

29. Stroke the hackle fibers back toward the hook bend and make a few turns of thread over their bases to hold them in place. Build a smooth thread head and whip-finish the thread. Remove the lead wire holding the legs in place at this time.

30. Clip both the front and back legs so they are about a hook length long. Peel a few fibers from the hackle collar across the top of the wing case to expose the flash a bit.

PATTERN VARIATIONS

JUMBO JOHN
(Black)

Hook:	Size 6–10 Tiemco 2499SP-BL
Bead:	Salmon-pink brass bead (3/16 inch)
Weight:	.020-inch-diameter lead wire
Thread:	Black 70- and 140-denier Ultra Thread
Tail:	Black goose biots
Abdomen:	Black Ultra Wire (medium)
Wing case:	Black Thin Skin and pearl saltwater Flashabou covered with epoxy
Thorax:	Natural Arizona synthetic peacock dubbing
Legs:	Black round rubber legs (medium)
Collar:	Black hen saddle

JUMBO JOHN
(Ginger/Black)

Hook:	Size 6–10 Tiemco 2499SP-BL
Bead:	Gold brass bead (3/16 inch)
Weight:	.020-inch-diameter lead wire
Thread:	Black 70- and 140-denier Ultra Thread
Tail:	Ginger goose biots
Abdomen:	Ginger and black Ultra Wire (medium)
Wing case:	Brown Thin Skin and pearl saltwater Flashabou covered with epoxy
Thorax:	Bronze Arizona synthetic peacock dubbing
Legs:	Pumpkin Sili Legs
Collar:	Mottled brown hen saddle

CHAPTER 5

Tung Teaser

Like the Copper John, the Tung Teaser is a heavily-weighted, all-purpose attractor pattern that doesn't represent any specific insect. I borrowed the color scheme from the time-proven Prince Nymph. I wanted to design a fly that looked a little more realistic than the Prince but still retained the fish-catching combination of peacock, brown, and white. In addition to having a more realistic profile than the Prince Nymph, the Tung Teaser is more durable. Real peacock herl is fragile and tends to fall apart after catching a few fish. The Tung Teaser's peacock color comes from a synthetic peacock dubbing that

CHARLIE CRAVEN

TUNG TEASER

Hook:	Size 8–18 Tiemco 5262
Thread:	Black 70-denier Ultra Thread
Bead:	Gold tungsten
Weight:	Lead wire (see chart)
Tail:	White goose biots
Rib:	Gold Ultra Wire (small)
Abdomen:	Bronze Arizona synthetic peacock dubbing
Wing case:	Mottled bustard Thin Skin and pearl Flashabou covered with epoxy
Thorax:	Bronze Arizona synthetic peacock dubbing
Legs:	Mottled brown hen-back fibers

Guides in Colorado use the Tung Teaser as a western green drake nymph. Rivers such as the Colorado, Roaring Fork, Blue, Frying Pan, and Rio Grande have excellent hatches. JOHN BARR

The Tung Teaser is an attractor pattern inspired by the venerable Prince Nymph. It catches fish on streams across the United States and works especially well as a generic drake or stonefly nymph. LANDON MAYER

has the same color as natural peacock herl when it is wet but lasts until you lose the fly.

Some Colorado guides use this fly as an imitation for the western green drake nymph. Green drake nymphs are large, nutritious food sources for trout, and they relish them. Green drakes hatch on many rivers across the country. In Colorado, we get excellent hatches on the Colorado, Roaring Fork, Blue, Frying Pan, Rio Grande, and many other rivers. They usually hatch sometime in July but can hatch into August depending on the river. Before the adult drakes hatch, the nymphs become active and many end up in the current flow,

becoming easy pickings for trout. The nymphs live in the riffles, so that is a good place to fish the Tung Teaser. Before a green drake hatch is an especially good time to dead-drift a size 12 Tung Teaser, but it will catch fish year-round. Feel free to give the indicator a little twitch with the rod tip during the drift.

I usually fish the Tung Teaser in a nymphing setup or as a second or third fly if using multiple nymphs. If it is green drake time I will fish it under a size 12 black Copper John. I use 3X fluorocarbon tied to both flies. It can also be a good choice to fish under a buoyant dry fly such as a B/C Hopper.

TUNG TEASER

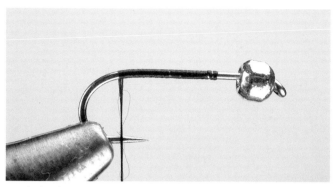

1. Slide the bead up to the eye of the hook. Insert the hook into the vise. Start the tying thread behind the bead and wrap a thread base back to the bend.

Hook Size	Lead Wire
8–12	.020 inch
14–16	.015 inch
18	.010 inch

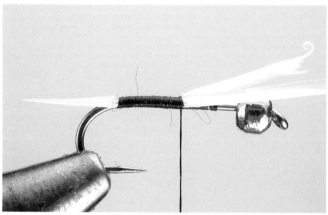

2. Oppose a pair of white goose biots so they curve away from each other and even their tips. Measure the biots against the hook so they are about one-half a shank length long. Tie the biots in at the bend of the hook and wrap forward over the butt ends to the midpoint on the shank, and then clip the excess biots.

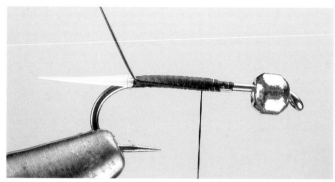

4. Wrap back over it with the thread to the base of the tail. Anchor the wire down tightly at the bend with several firm turns of thread.

5. Apply some dubbing to the thread and build a tapered abdomen from the base of the tail to the 70 percent point on the shank.

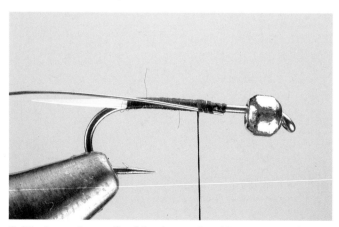

3. Tie in a piece of gold wire at the 60 percent point on the shank.

6. The body should have an even taper.

on the surface of a river is unpredictable. However, if you see a lot of shucks along the bank, and you see some adult stoneflies flying around, blind fishing an appropriate adult pattern can be effective. Some of the trout have undoubtedly seen a big juicy adult on the water and are keeping an eye out for them.

Some species hatch in the river, most notably the yellow sally, a common name for a wide range of small stoneflies with colors ranging from yellow to chartreuse. The sally that is most common in Colorado where I fish is a small, yellowish stonefly imitated with a pattern tied on a size 16 standard hook. Standard dry-fly hook sizes 14–20 will cover most sallies, with 16 being one of the most common sizes. They are widespread and often produce excellent dry-fly fishing with adult patterns. Many species of yellow sallies hatch in the river, and the trout see lots of adults on the water. I have seen yellow sally nymphs floating downstream in the surface film and watched as the dun split the nymphal shuck and hatched.

When anglers think of stonefly nymphs, they often imagine the large, fully mature stage of some of the larger species. When you pick up a rock and check out the nymphs, many times you are looking at immature specimens. Stonefly nymphs of each species come in all sizes and even the large salmonfly nymph, which can grow to almost the size of your little finger, starts out small. It takes them three to four years to attain their mature size. Smaller sizes of dark stones (10–14) can be effective in a river with a good population of salmonfly nymphs.

The second fly-tying book I owned was Polly Rosborough's *Tying and Fishing the Fuzzy Nymph*. The first stonefly nymphs I tied and used were Polly's pattern. His pattern used teal flank feathers died brown or golden for the tail, back, wing case, and legs. The body was yarn and ribbed with thread. They were effective, and the pattern I tie today incorporates the general theme of his pattern, but is embellished with some changes, modern synthetics, and other natural materials.

Though the naturals come in a wide variety of colors, dark brown and golden colors cover most of the stoneflies that I see on stream. The color doesn't need to be exact, just close enough. Stonefly nymphs like to live in highly-oxygenated riffles and sometimes in deep, fast moving water, so I add both a tungsten bead and lead to help the fly sink quickly.

I tie both Flashback and plain versions. I primarily fish stonefly nymph patterns in the spring and early summer. That is when most stoneflies hatch, so that is when their nymphs are most active and available to the trout. I usually end up fishing the flashback version. It works well, and often in the spring and early summer,

This brown trout gobbled a size 10 Flashback Dark Tungstone. There were no adult stoneflies in the air, but because the nymphs are available in different sizes to trout all year long, a stonefly imitation is a good choice. LANDON MAYER

Golden stonefly nymph. DAVE HUGHES

This large (approximately 14 pounds) Great Lakes brown trout fell for a size 14 Flashback Golden Tungstone. JOHN BARR

you can have off-colored water. I carry both the dark and golden versions in sizes 8–16. Unlike many mayflies and caddis, which have a one-year life cycle, many of the larger golden and dark stones have a two- to four-year cycle, so even if the hatch is over, there are still plenty of immature stonefly nymphs of various sizes in the river throughout the year. In rivers with good stonefly nymph populations, trout see a lot of stonefly nymphs of all sizes, so they generally are not picky about size. Though I usually fish stonefly nymphs in spring and summer, they can be effective throughout the year. I have heard that for many anglers across the country, stoneflies are go-to patterns in the fall and winter.

I fish the Tungstone in a typical nymph setup with an indicator. I usually fish three flies, with the Tungstone the last fly so that it is as close to the bottom as possible. The lightest tippet I use with stonefly nymphs is 4X, but most of the time I use 3X fluorocarbon. The Tungstone is so heavy I often don't need split shot to get to the bottom except when fishing deep runs with fast-flowing currents.

SALMONFLIES AND
THE DARK TUNGSTONE

Salmonflies are the largest stoneflies in the country. It is spectacular to see large numbers of adults fluttering around. Salmonflies entice some of the largest fish in the river to feed on both the huge nymphs and the careless egg-laying females that end up in the water. The mature nymphs can be two inches or larger and the adults can be the size of a large dragonfly with a fat black-orange body and orange wings. Many large trout like a large meal because they get more nutrition for the energy expended than if they were going after smaller food sources.

Large trout are primarily carnivores, feeding on other fish and crawdads, and they often feed nocturnally, making them unavailable to daytime fishermen. Due to their size, salmonflies are one of the few aquatic insects that will cause the largest fish in the river to switch from their fish and crawdad diet to aquatic insects, and to feed during the day on the adult females that end up on the water's surface.

For instance, the only time of the year anglers consistently catch monster trout in the Black Canyon of the Gunnison is when salmonflies are hatching. Fly fishers drift downstream looking for water stains on the rock walls, which indicate where a trout has taken a natural with a slashing rise. Put a fly upstream of the splash mark and you just about have a guaranteed take.

Pteronarcys species can be found from the east to west coast but are most numerous in some of the larger western rivers such as the Madison, Big Hole, Gunnison, and the Colorado. The dark Tungstone in a size 6 or 8 will catch these fish even though the naturals may be a size 2 or 1/0. Trout do not seem to be selective about size when it comes to the large stonefly nymphs. I think it is because there are three to four age classes of the nymphs in the river, and the trout see many sizes of the naturals. The nymphs become active as they are getting ready to crawl out of the river and trout will keep an eye out for them when they leave their hiding places. Pre-hatch fishing with the nymphs can be excellent.

I have chased salmonfly hatches all over the West, and I have rarely had good dry-fly fishing with adult patterns when the air was thick with adult salmonflies. This was always an enigma to me, until Mike Lawson provided me with a plausible explanation. The nymphs crawl out of the river late in the evening, at night or very early in the morning and the trout may gorge themselves on the nymphs and are stuffed the following

Salmonfly nymph. DAVE HUGHES

Stoneflies thrive in fast, oxygenated water. Though many anglers concentrate on deep runs, shallower areas can be good places to fish a Tungstone when the stoneflies are migrating toward shore. Fish a Tungstone under a dry fly or indicator and modify the length of tippet to adjust the depth at which you fish the pattern, depending on water conditions.

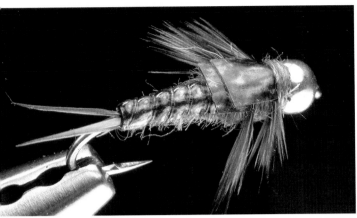

CHARLIE CRAVEN

FLASHBACK TUNGSTONE
(Dark)

Hook:	Size 6–14 Tiemco 5263
Bead:	Golden tungsten
Thread:	Brown 6/0 Danville
Weight:	Lead wire (see chart)
Tail:	Brown goose biots
Rib:	3X monofilament
Flashback:	Pearl Lateral Scale
Shellback:	Mottled oak Thin Skin, natural color
Abdomen:	Brown Wapsi Sow Scud dubbing
Wing case:	Mottled oak Thin Skin, natural color
Thorax:	Brown Wapsi Sow Scud dubbing
Legs:	Brown-dyed grizzly hen saddle

day. Salmonflies start hatching in a particular stretch of river and every day the hatch moves upstream. My idea at the time of our conversation was to fish an adult pattern several days after the naturals have hatched on a particular stretch of a river. The nymphs would have left the river, and that big nutritious meal would still be imprinted in the minds of the fish. The good dry-fly fishing I've had probably occurred several days after the hatch had passed through.

GOLDEN STONEFLIES AND THE GOLDEN TUNGSTONE

Goldens are found from coast to coast but are most prominent in the West, from the Rocky Mountains to the Pacific coast. Like the dark stoneflies, the nymph is the most important stage of the insect for anglers. The nymphs are large and can reach lengths of one to two inches. They are various shades of light to dark gold. Like their dark counterparts, the nymphs of most goldens crawl out of the river very late in the evening, at night, and very early in the morning.

I fished a stretch of the Yampa River outside of Steamboat, Colorado, in spring 2002 for two days. The first day the rocks were clean, and the second day many of the rocks were covered with large golden stonefly shucks. There were adults flying around and they had obviously hatched the night before. The fishing was significantly slower the second day than the first day. My guess is the fish had been eating the migrating nymphs all night.

Golden stone nymphs are common trout foods in streams across the country. Golden stonefly patterns are deadly in the summer when golden stoneflies are hatching, and many anglers fish them in the winter and early spring, when a large stonefly nymph is not a meal that a hungry trout would pass up.

JOHN BARR

In a river that contains golden stones, a Golden Tungstone is a good option all year long. The nymphs take two to three years to mature, so there are always some nymphs in the river. In my opinion the golden stones don't get the notoriety that the salmonflies get because they aren't as impressive looking, and the timing of the hatch is less predictable. I think that many a large yellow-bodied Stimulator is taken as an adult golden stone.

TUNGSTONE

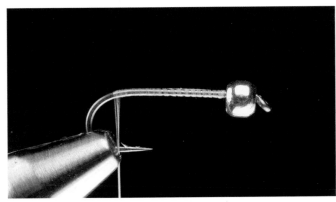

1. Put the bead on the hook and slide it up to the hook eye. Insert the hook into the vise. Start the tying thread right behind the bead and wrap back to the bend, forming a smooth thread base as you go.

HOOK SIZE	LEAD WIRE
8–14	.020 inch
16	.015 inch
18	.010 inch

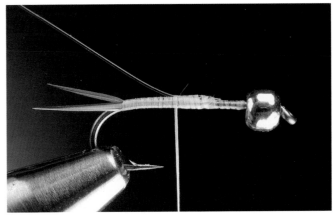

3. Tie in a length of 3X tippet material at the midpoint of the shank on the far side of the hook. Wrap back over the mono to the base of the tail.

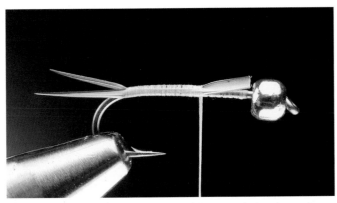

2. Cut and oppose two goose biots and tie them in at the bend of the hook so the pointed ends extend past the bend of the hook about one-half a shank length. Wrap forward over the butt ends to the midpoint on the shank and clip the excess.

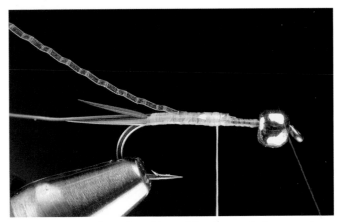

4. Return the thread to the midpoint and tie in a piece of pearl Lateral Scale flash. Make sure to keep the flash flat on top of the hook shank and wrap back over it to the base of the tail as well.

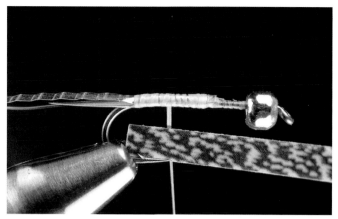

5. Cut a strip of Thin Skin that is about half the width of the hook gap.

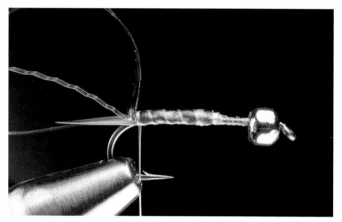

6. Tie the Thin Skin in at the midpoint of the shank and wrap back over it to the bend. Stretching the Thin Skin as you wrap over it will help to keep it centered and cupped around the hook.

7. Dub the abdomen to the 65 percent point on the hook, forming a slight taper.

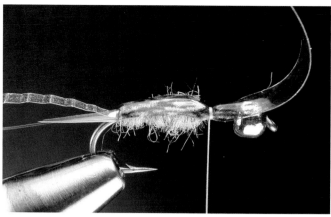

8. Pull the Thin Skin shellback over the top of the abdomen and tie it down at the front.

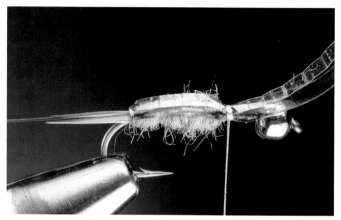

9. Pull the Lateral Scale forward over the top of the Thin Skin, taking care to keep it centered as well, and tie it down at the front.

10. Rib the 3X tippet material forward through the abdomen about five or six turns, and tie off the mono at the front. Clip the excess Thin Skin, flash, and mono at this point. Begin dubbing the thorax with a small ball of dubbing right up to, and even slightly overlapping, the abdomen.

11. Select a gold-dyed grizzly hen saddle feather.

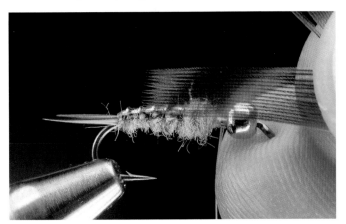

12. Preen a small bunch of hackle fibers out from the stem of the feather so the tips are even.

13. Tie this clump of hackle fibers in on the far side of the hook so they extend back to the hook point and are in line with the hook shank.

14. Tie another equal-size clump of hackle fibers in along the near side of the hook in the same manner. Clip the butt ends of both clumps flush against the shank.

15. Take the remaining piece of Thin Skin leftover from the abdomen backstrap and cut the end straight across. Lay this piece on top of the first thorax section as shown here. The wing case should cover the first thorax segment as well as the very front edge of the abdomen.

16. Bind the Thin Skin wing case in place with a couple turns of thread.

17. The Thin Skin should buckle evenly around the hook shank and cup against the thorax dubbing. Clip the excess Thin Skin, but save the stub for the second wing case.

18. Dub the second thoracic section up to just behind the bead.

19. Tie in another clump of fibers on the far side of the hook.

20. Tie in a clump on the near side.

21. Clip the end of the reserved piece of Thin Skin square once again and tie it in at the front edge of the second thoracic segment as you did with the first one.

22. The second segment tied in. Clip the excess Thin Skin as close to the bead as you can.

23. Dub a small collar right behind the bead to cover the tie-off area. Whip-finish and clip the thread.

25. Golden Tungstone, wet.

24. Finished fly.

CHAPTER 7

Cranefly Larva

Craneflies are related to midges and mosquitoes and live in trout waters throughout the United States. The larvae range in size from ½ inch to almost 3 inches, can be cream to olive to gray in color, and look like fat midge larvae. The adults look like giant mosquitoes with extra long legs. The larvae of the larger species are long and thick-bodied, offering bountiful, nutritious meals for trout. It takes hundreds of midge larvae to equal the food value of one large cranefly larva, and it requires a lot less effort to take one bite instead of hundreds.

Craneflies are different from other aquatic trout foods in that many larvae live in the soil along the stream, though a number also live in the river and riverbanks. The ones that live in streams inhabit a variety of stream bottoms and all the different current types, from slow runs to riffles. Tailwaters often have robust populations of cranefly larvae.

The most important phase of the cranefly for fly fishers is the larva. The terrestrial cranefly larvae pupate in the soil, but the aquatic cranefly larvae pupate on land as well, deep in riverbanks where they are unavailable to trout. The adults also hatch on the riverbank. Adults spend a lot of time in streamside vegetation or on the ground. The only time trout see the adults is when the females are laying their eggs out over the water. The problem for fly fishermen is that the egg laying is done most often at night or very early in the morning. If the flows are static, aquatic cranefly larvae generally remain buried in silt or under rocks or wood. They do not drift like most aquatic insects.

Cranefly larvae do become an important food source if the flows increase: during spring runoff, after a rain that raises the river, or when a reservoir bumps up the water release. The increased water flow can dislodge larvae from both the bottom of the river and the stream-banks. A cranefly larva pattern can be an excellent choice during these high water conditions, although I have caught many trout on a cranefly larva when there was no rising water.

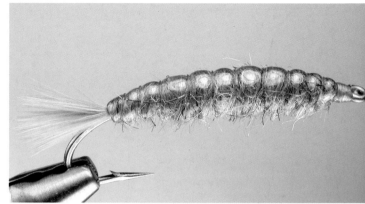

CHARLIE CRAVEN

CRANEFLY LARVA
(Olive)

Hook:	Size 6–8 Tiemco 200R
Weight:	.020-inch-diameter lead wire
Thread:	Olive 70-denier Ultra Thread
Tail:	Pale olive-gray marabou
Rib:	3X tippet material
Shellback:	Tan Thin Skin
Body:	Gray-olive Arizona synthetic dubbing

"No box is complete on the North Platte (outside of Casper, Wyoming) without Barr's Cranefly Larva. We have a fairly high flow here in the late spring and summer, which washes a lot of the cranefly larvae out of the bank and from the river bottom. Barr's Crane is key. We smash lots of big fish on this fly and it's our go-to bug in high water. Nymphing it deep or in fast shallow riffles, it doesn't seem to matter."

—Jason Hamrick, Cowboy Drifters, Casper, Wyoming

Years ago, during the 1970s when my home water was the South Platte in the Deckers area in Colorado, the Cranefly Larva was one of my favorite patterns. Some of the bait fishermen would use what they referred to as "rock worms." Years later I realized that the rock worms were cranefly larvae. After one of the guys showed me his bait container holding fat grubs that he had gotten out of the river, I tied a pattern resembling a rock worm. It was tied on a long-shank hook and had a body of dubbed beaver fur. The pattern worked great and became one of my favorites. In later years, I tied a bead-head pattern with olive dubbing and a black ostrich herl collar.

For some reason, I forgot about cranefly larva patterns. With all of the new patterns coming out every year we tend to forget about some of the old ones. In fall 2002, I was floating the North Platte River outside of Casper, Wyoming. I kept seeing large cranefly adults crawling around on the riverbank. These were most likely freshly hatched from the stream bank. I recalled how the Cranefly Larva used to be one of my best patterns, and I decided to resurrect it using new materials.

The pattern I use now differs from my earlier rendition. It is tied in sizes 6 and 8. Although the naturals come in smaller and larger sizes, I tie the fly only in these two sizes for simplicity's sake and because they seem to work the best. Naturals come in a variety of colors, but a tannish cream and a gray olive cover most of the bases. Many existing cranefly larva patterns have a dark head, but these patterns do not accurately represent the natural. After doing some research, I discovered that the naturals do have a dark head but keep their head retracted inside their body when being carried by the

I caught this monster on the North Platte in Wyoming. Craneflies are an overlooked food source. During high water, many cranefly larvae are dislodged from the streambank and bottom, and trout are on the lookout for them. If you are fishing a river that contains cranefly larvae, and there is rising water or if there has been high water, this pattern can be a good choice. JOHN BARR

Cranefly larva. DAVE HUGHES

Cranefly adult. DAVE HUGHES

While adult cranes—they look like very big mosquitos—can provide sporadic opportunities to catch trout on the surface, trout feed on cranefly larvae more consistently. JOHN BARR

current. A real cranefly larva is uniform in color without the appearance of a head. Cranefly larvae don't have a true tail but they do have some short appendages on the end of their body called lobes, which I represent with a small clump of marabou clipped to about ¼ inch.

All winter and early spring the North Platte near Casper flows around 500 cfs (cubic feet per second). Every spring the dam operators crank up the flows to about 4000–5000 cfs to flush out all of the dead aquatic vegetation from the previous year. In spring 2003 I fished the river shortly after a flush. Upon arriving at a good run, I rigged up and tied on my new Cranefly Larva. I had very little confidence in it but had to try it. I started catching fish at a good pace and even managed a stretch where I caught six fish on six casts.

A logical explanation for the fly's success was that the high water had dislodged many cranefly larvae from the streambank and the bottom, and trout were on the lookout for them. If you are fishing a river that contains cranefly larva, and there is rising water or if there has been high water, this pattern can be a good choice.

One of the reasons we don't think about craneflies is that we don't often see them. I was reading Mike Lawson's outstanding book, *Spring Creeks*, and in it he said he has seen very little cranefly adult egg laying during the

day. Craneflies hatch from the riverbank, and the adults spend most of their time crawling around in the streamside vegetation and on the ground. Most hatch at night and most females lay their eggs out over the water at night or early in the morning. They skitter along the surface dropping their eggs and the fish rise for them vigorously. I have seen one such event and was totally unprepared for it. I had no large dries that I could skitter along the surface.

Just the other day I was in Charlie's Fly Box in Arvada, Colorado. A fellow who works for him, Dave Ziegman, had been up on the Dream Stream—the South Platte between Spinney and Elevenmile Reservoirs—and saw lots of cranes laying eggs. Many big browns, up out of Elevenmile Reservoir to spawn, were in a total feeding frenzy, viciously slashing at the skittering cranefly adults. The way Dave described it reminded me of roosterfish ripping into bait. Dave had some large Stimulators and did catch some quality fish skating the pattern through some runs. I have fished the Dream Stream hundreds of times and never witnessed this phenomenon.

A friend of mine, Ritchie Montella, used to guide on the Beaverhead River outside of Dillon, Montana, and kept a running total of all the big browns that he caught on a piece of paper that he kept in his wallet to show people. There were many 8-pound-plus browns written down on that paper. Ritchie fished at night under a full moon. He would use 0X tippet and a big, heavily-hackled pattern that he skated across the surface to mimic the skittering behavior of the adult egg-laying female craneflies. He knew the river and was often able to time when the adult craneflies would begin their egg-laying flights. He said the technique still worked even if there were no naturals present. A cranefly larva pattern would probably be a good nymph in the Beaverhead.

I most often fish the Cranefly Larva with an indicator. It is usually my top fly, and if I am catching fish on it, I also use it as my second fly. I fish both colors, one a size 6, the other a size 8. I always use 3X fluorocarbon for my tippet. With the whole shank wrapped with lead, the fly is very heavy and I usually do not use split shot.

CRANEFLY LARVA

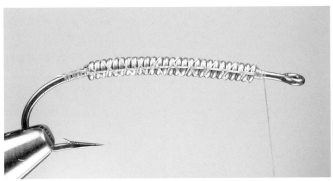

1. Place the hook in the vise and make about thirty wraps of large lead wire around the shank. The lead should stop a couple eye lengths back from the hook eye and run back to just short of the hook bend. Start the tying thread in front of the lead wire and build a slight taper up to the lead. Wrap the thread back over the lead wraps to the bend of the hook, forming a smooth thread base. Return the thread to the front of the lead wraps. You don't need to completely cover the lead wraps with thread, just cross-wrap to anchor the lead in place.

2. Clump the tip of an olive gray marabou feather together into a bunch and measure the tip so it is about as long as the gap of the hook. Tie the clump in at the bend of the hook with the tip extending out the rear of the hook.

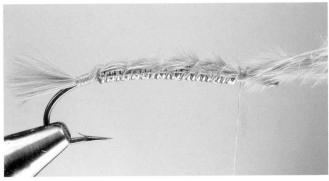

3. Pull the remaining butt end of the marabou feather forward over the top of the shank and wrap the thread forward over it to just behind the hook eye. This allows the bulk of the marabou to create a smooth underbody on the shank.

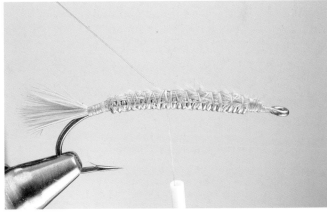

4. Clip the remaining butt end of the marabou flush at the eye. Wrap the thread back over the marabou underbody to smooth it out a bit. Return the tying thread to the front of the hook and tie in a length of tippet material for the rib. Tie the tippet in on the far side of the hook and wrap back over it to the bend, and then return the thread to mid-shank.

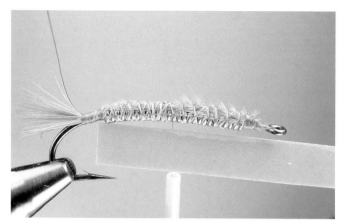

5. Cut a strip of Thin Skin that is just a bit narrower than the hook gap. Peel the paper backing from the Thin Skin strip.

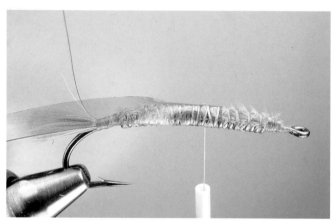

6. Lay the Thin Skin on top of the hook shank at the midpoint of the hook and fold it around the hook. Tie the Thin Skin down tightly at the front end with a few firm wraps of thread.

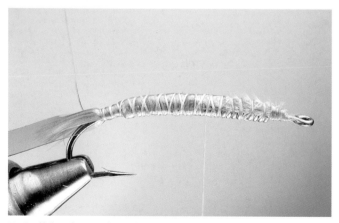

7. Pull back on the Thin Skin to stretch it slightly and continue wrapping back over it to the base of the tail. Stretching the Thin Skin in this manner will allow it to cup around the shank and buckle into position for the shellback.

8. Dub the thread heavily and begin forming a tapered body from the bend of the hook. Dub half the body first with one strand of dubbing, then come back and add more dubbing for the front half, rather than trying to turn a foot-long strand of dubbing around the hook.

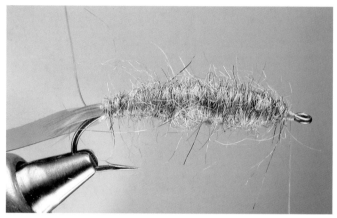

9. Add more dubbing to the thread and complete an elongated, football-shaped body. The body should be fattest in the middle and taper down at either end.

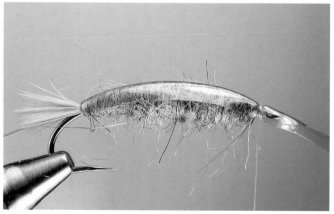

10. Pull the Thin Skin forward over the body and tie it down right behind the eye. Take care to let the Thin Skin buckle over the top of the dubbing, cupping the dubbing underneath. Do not clip the Thin Skin just yet.

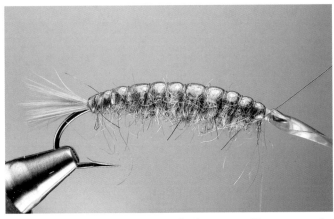

11. Rib through the body with the monofilament, making about a dozen evenly-spaced turns. Pull tightly on the tippet material to sink it down into the body and create prominent segments.

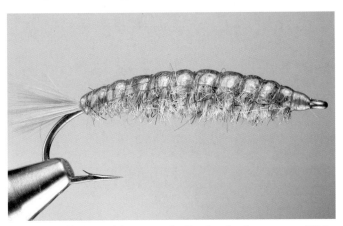

12. Tie off the ribbing and clip both the excess Thin Skin and ribbing material flush against the hook eye. Build a smoothly-tapered thread head with the tying thread and whip-finish. Clip the thread. Trim the dubbing across the bottom of the fly a bit to smooth out the body shape. Place a drop of head cement on the thread head.

13. Cranefly, wet.

PATTERN VARIATION

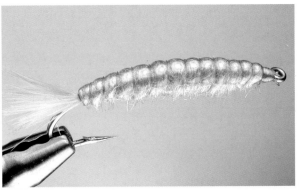

CHARLIE CRAVEN

CRANEFLY LARVA
(Cream)

Hook:	Size 6–8 Tiemco 200R
Weight:	.020-inch-diameter lead wire
Thread:	Tan 3/0 monocord
Tail:	Pale tan marabou
Rib:	3X tippet material
Shellback:	Tan Thin Skin
Body:	Tan Arizona synthetic dubbing

CHAPTER 8

Uncased and Cased Caddis Larva

Caddisflies are one of the most common and widespread of all aquatic insects. There are approximately 1,400 species of caddisflies, outnumbering the total amount of mayfly and stonefly species combined. They are found in both flowing and still waters. Caddis are also the most tolerant of polluted water and higher water temperatures, making them critical insects in marginal or seasonal trout streams.

Every fly fisher has seen the little mothlike adults flying around streams and near bankside vegetation. Fishermen always talk about hatches, because that is what produces the most glamorous and fun fishing. The reality is that most of a trout's caddisfly diet is the larva, and during a "hatch," trout feed on more pupae than actual adults. In my opinion, along with the cranefly larva, the caddis larva is one of the most underused patterns.

Caddisflies undergo a complete metamorphosis—egg, larva, pupa, and adult. Like all aquatic insects, the larva or nymph stage is the longest stage of their life cycle, which, for most species, lasts about one year. A few species have two cycles a year, and a few others have a two-year cycle, but most live for one year, with the larvae spending about eight or nine months in the river. The larva range in size from ⅛ to 2 inches or more and come in various shades of cream, green, and brown.

Most caddisfly larvae prefer to live in highly oxygenated riffles, though some can live in slower water. The population of some species in a river can be staggering, resulting in blizzardlike hatches. In addition to the abundance of caddisfly larvae, one of the reasons they are such an important trout food is their propensity to regularly drift in the water's currents. Aquatic insects drift in the current for two reasons. The first is called a behavioral drift, whereby the insects let go of their hold on the rocks and other debris on the stream bottom and drift in the current until they land on something they can hold on to. Most aquatic insects are poor swimmers and are at the whims of the current and bottom structure. Some entomologists say that the insects drift because their original home has become overpopulated and they are looking for a better feeding area, or that it is

CHARLIE CRAVEN

CASED CADDIS LARVA
(Green)

Hook:	Size 12–16 Tiemco 5262 or 2302
Bead:	Black tungsten (see chart)
Weight:	.015-inch-diameter lead wire
Thread:	Black 8/0 Uni-Thread
Case:	Brown Arizona synthetic dubbing
Shellback:	Olive flyspecks Thin Skin
Thorax:	Caddis green Nature's Spirit Emergence dubbing
Legs:	Black ostrich herl

just part of their intrinsic behavior. Trout see and eat lots of them.

Behavioral drift occurs most often in low light (late or early in the day or at night), but can happen midday. The only drift I have seen occurred in the early afternoon on the Colorado River below State Bridge, Colorado. There were thousands of cased caddis drifting downstream just below the surface and the trout fed on them feverishly. Cased caddis are one of the few aquatic insects that will behaviorally drift during the day.

The second type of drifting is involuntary and is called catastrophic drift. This type of drift occurs

Caddisflies can be broken into two groups: those that build cases and those that do not. Green and Tan Cased Caddis (bottom right) and Uncased Caddis Larvae cover most of the basis for subsurface caddis imitations. CHARLIE CRAVEN

when the water rises and dislodges the insects or if they lose their grip while crawling around and the current carries them downstream. Fishing a caddis larva during rising water conditions can be a very effective approach.

Most caddisfly larvae fall into one of three categories: net spinners, free-living, and cased caddis. The net spinners comprise almost half of all caddis species. They get their name because they spin a spiderweb-like seine that covers their hiding spot, which is a little crevice in a rock or stick. The web traps food particles of various stream detritus (mostly plant debris and algae) from the current flow, which the larvae eat. The free-living caddis just crawl around the bottom looking for food (they are omnivorous), making themselves readily available to trout and susceptible to being dislodged. They frequently get swept from the bottom by the current and float helplessly until they can find a new spot to latch on to.

The cased caddis build a shell around their bodies from sand and detritus in the water. They attach themselves to rocks and sticks with a silk-like material. They leave an opening at one end so that they can stick their heads out to feed. You can pick a stick out of some rivers, and sometimes the entire stick is covered with cased caddis.

You need to seine the river for the free livers, and look at rocks and wood to check out the net spinners and cased larvae to see what size they are. Remember,

Net-spinning caddis. DAVE HUGHES

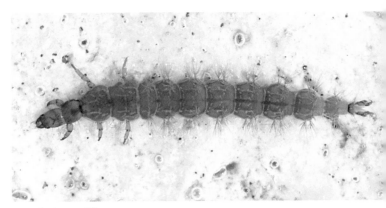

Free-living caddis. DAVE HUGHES

Caddis hatch from spring through fall, so a caddis larva is always a good choice when nymph-fishing. Most caddis prefer highly-oxygenated water, so concentrate on fishing riffles and other broken water. LANDON MAYER

Case-building caddis. DAVE HUGHES

most caddis larvae have a one-year cycle, and the size of the larvae will vary from month to month as they grow.

I tied my first Caddis Larva in the 1980s after seining the Colorado River. All of the larvae were some shade of green, olive, or tan. Through the years I have caught a lot of fish on caddis larva imitations. I tie two caddis larva patterns. The uncased version represents both the net spinner and free-living caddis equally well. There are hundreds of species of uncased caddis larvae, most of which range in color from green to tan. The pattern went through numerous changes to reach its present version. Natural caddis larvae have little appendages on the rear of their body, so I started the pattern with a short little tuft of Z-lon. The bodies are distinctly segmented so I ribbed the dubbed body with monofilament. I added a strip of a Ziploc bag back (since replaced by Thin Skin) on the top of the abdomen, thorax, and head, which made the fly look more like a real larva. Because the naturals have a darker head and thorax than abdomen, I darkened those portions of dubbing with a marking pen and added three wraps of dark ostrich herl to represent legs.

To create the Cased Caddis Larva, dub some brown dubbing on the rear two-thirds of the hook and make the front third the same as the head and thorax portion of the Uncased Caddis Larva. Although there are larger and smaller naturals, sizes 10 through 16 should cover most of the bases. I don't think trout get selective about size when eating caddis larvae because there are so many different sizes in a river. There are numerous species that come in a variety of sizes, and there are both mature and immature larvae. If a particular major hatch, like the Mother's Day hatch, is right around the corner, then you should match the size and color of the mature caddis larva that is going to pupate and hatch into the adult.

I was fishing the Roaring Fork River near Basalt, Colorado, about fifteen years ago with two good friends: noted artist Dave Hall and Van Rollo. At the time I didn't understand caddis entomology very well, but I knew the Roaring Fork had great caddis hatches. It was a bluebird day and nothing was hatching. We were nymph-fishing some riffles with green Uncased Caddis Larvae and catching fish right and left. It was far more effective than any other pattern. The logical explanation why the pattern worked so well is that caddis hatches were coming up soon; the caddis larvae were probably getting active before pupating, and the trout were keying in on them.

Before the larvae pupate they become active, often getting swept into the current flow where the trout keep an eye out for them and readily eat them. Fishing an appropriate caddis larva 4 to 8 weeks before a hatch can produce some outstanding fishing. Trout eat them while they are maturing, but when larvae become very active before pupating, fishing a larva pattern can be especially effective. The pupae are cocooned up and hidden away from trout, and are not a factor before the hatch. The pupa stage lasts about a month before they begin to hatch. Because of their often huge populations in a river, and that caddis hatch from spring through fall, a caddis larva is always a good choice when nymph-fishing.

Most net spinners and free-living larvae like highly-oxygenated water, so concentrate on fishing riffles and other broken water. I most often fish this fly as part of a nymphing setup. It can be any of the flies in a two- or three-fly setup, but I usually fish it as the bottom fly. It can also be the bottom nymph when fishing Hopper-Copper-Dropper. I will use 4 or 5X fluorocarbon tippet most of the time. Generally I like a dead drift, but a little twitch here and there is fine. The larva is alive and can squirm and move while it is drifting.

CASED CADDIS LARVA

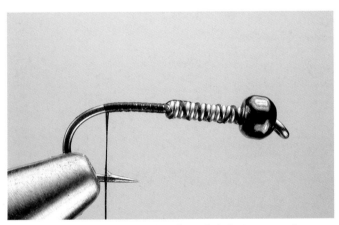

1. Place the bead on the hook and slide it up to the eye. Insert the hook into the vise. Make fifteen to twenty turns of lead wire on the shank, break the ends off, and shove the lead wraps up into the back of the bead. Start the tying thread behind the lead wraps. Make a thread base over the lead wraps and back again to the bend of the hook.

2. Dub a slightly-tapered case about two-thirds of the way up the hook shank.

HOOK SIZE	BEAD
12	$1/8$ inch
14–16	$7/64$ inch

3. Cut a strip of Thin Skin that is about half as wide as the hook gap. Remove the paper backing and tie the Thin Skin in at the front edge of the dubbing on top of the hook.

4. Tie in a single strand of ostrich herl by its butt end at the front of the dubbing.

5. Dub a level section of green dubbing right up to the back of the bead.

7. Pull the Thin Skin over the tip of the green dubbing and ostrich herl and tie it down at the back of the bead.

6. Make a wide turn to the front of the green dubbing with the ostrich herl, then make a couple more closely-spaced turns at the front. Tie off the ostrich herl behind the bead.

8. Clip the Thin Skin flush against the bead. Make a few tight turns of thread to cover the stub end and whip-finish.

UNCASED CADDIS LARVA

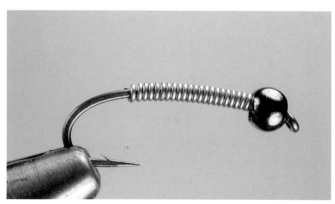

1. Place the bead on the hook and slide it up to the eye. Insert the hook into the vise. Make about twenty wraps of lead wire around the shank, break off the stub ends, and shove the wraps up into the bead.

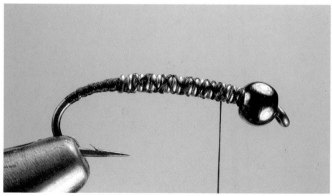

2. Start the tying thread at the back edge of the lead wraps and form a smooth thread base back to the bend. Wrap the thread forward over the lead wraps to anchor them in place.

3. Tie in a clump of Z-lon just behind the bead and wrap back over it to the bend of the hook. Return the thread to the front of the hook.

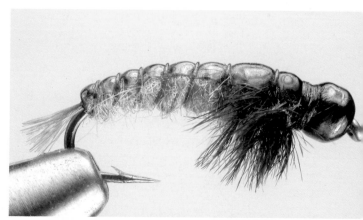

CHARLIE CRAVEN

UNCASED CADDIS LARVA
(Green)

Hook:	Size 12–16 Tiemco 2302
Bead:	Black (see chart)
Weight:	.015-inch-diameter lead wire
Thread:	Black 8/0 Uni-Thread
Tail Stub:	Olive Z-lon
Rib:	3X monofilament
Shellback:	Olive flyspecks Thin Skin
Body:	Caddis green Nature's Spirit Emergence dubbing
Thorax:	Black ostrich herl

4. Tie in a 6-inch length of 3X mono along the far side of the hook shank.

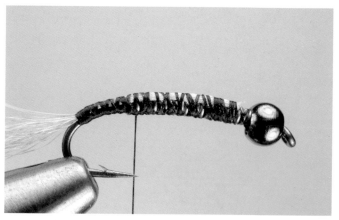

5. Wrap back over the mono to the bend of the hook, keeping it along the far side of the shank as you wrap.

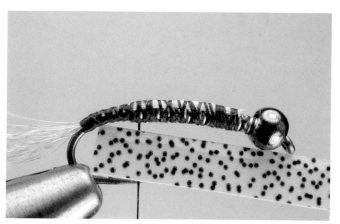

6. Cut a strip of Thin Skin that is about as wide as the hook gap. Remove the paper backing from the Thin Skin.

7. Tie the Thin Skin in at the back edge of the lead wraps. Pull the Thin Skin taut as you wrap back over it to the bend.

8. Dub a robust, slightly tapered body all the way up to the back edge of the bead.

9. Move the thread back over the front edge of the dubbing about one-quarter of a shank length. Tie in a single strand of ostrich herl by its butt end, and return the thread to the back of the bead.

10. Spiral wrap the ostrich herl up to the bead and tie it off. Clip the excess ostrich herl flush.

11. Pull the Thin Skin shellback over the top of the dubbed body and ostrich herl and tie it down at the back edge of the bead.

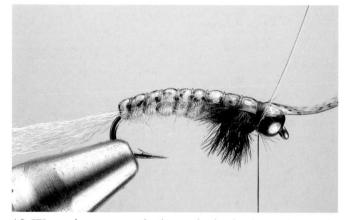

12. Wrap the mono rib through the body with evenly spaced turns. Pull tightly on the mono so it bites into the dubbing and creates prominent segments. When you reach the back edge of the ostrich, use the mono to divide the thorax section in half, making a single turn through the center of the ostrich herl. Tie off and clip the mono and Thin Skin at the back edge of the bead.

13. Make a few tight turns of thread to cover the butt ends and whip-finish.

14. Close-up of Uncased Caddis Larva before marking with a pen.

15. Darken the last two segments of Thin Skin with a black marker.

16. The finished fly.

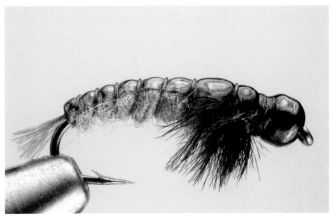

17. Green version.

18. Tan Uncased Caddis Larva, wet.

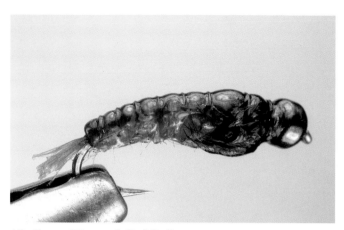

19. Green Uncased Caddis Larva, wet.

PATTERN VARIATION

CHARLIE CRAVEN

UNCASED CADDIS LARVA (Tan)

Hook: Size 12–16 Tiemco 2302
Bead: Black (see chart)
Weight: .015-inch-diameter lead wire
Thread: Black 8/0 Uni-Thread
Tail Stub: Cream Z-lon
Rib: 3X monofilament
Shellback: Tan flyspecks Thin Skin
Body: Tan Wapsi Sow Scud dubbing
Thorax: Black ostrich herl

CHAPTER 9

Graphic Caddis

Wherever there are caddis larvae, there are caddis pupae. Caddis will hatch spring through fall, so trout get accustomed to seeing the pupae and readily accept them as a tasty treat, whether caddis are hatching or not. Unless there is a hatch in progress, trout feed opportunistically and will eat a wide variety of foods.

After eight or nine months, the caddis larvae pupate for about a month. Throughout that month they gradually transform into fully mature pupae, ready to hatch into adults. While they are pupating, they are hidden from trout and are not available as a food source. Once they are mature and get ready to emerge, they become an extremely important food source.

Many believe that when ready to hatch, caddis pupae rocket to the surface like Polaris missiles, but they actually drift downriver in the current before swimming to the surface (the drift can be anywhere from five feet to a long distance). Trout eagerly gobble them up when they are drifting like this. When they are ready, the pupae swim to the surface and emerge into adults. While they are ascending the water column, they are also vulnerable and are readily eaten by trout. The pupae are powerful and fast swimmers after they have drifted for a while. As they near the surface or are on the surface, trout can be aggressive in their take and produce slashy riseforms, which are good indicators that trout may be feeding on pupae.

Even when there is no hatch, if you see adult caddis flying around, or shake some bushes and see numerous caddis come flying out, you know there has been a hatch and the trout have seen and eaten many pupae. One evening in fall 2003 I was on the North Platte River near Alcova, Wyoming, and there were a number of large fish rising on a big flat. The only insects on the water were size 26 adult Tricos (one of the few times I have seen adult Tricos hatching in the evening). The hatch was heavy, so with all the competition from the naturals and difficulty in seeing a tiny fly in the low light, I knew I had a slim chance of hooking the trout with a size 26 dun pattern. I had seen large numbers of adult caddis swarming around the river, but not on the water. I fig-

CHARLIE CRAVEN

GRAPHIC CADDIS
(Olive)

Hook:	Size 14–16 Tiemco 2499SP-BL
Thread:	Olive 6/0 Danville
Abdomen:	Olive Wapsi stretch tubing
Tag:	Silver holographic Flashabou
Legs:	Brown Hungarian partridge body feather fibers
Head:	Natural gray ostrich

ured that they had to have hatched in the river at some point, so the trout obviously had seen numerous pupae. The adult caddis were light tan, so I tied on a size 16 tan Graphic Caddis and started swinging into the riseforms. If the trout were feeding selectively on the Trico duns, I had no chance. It turns out they were not. Just about every fish that saw my fly took it. Though the fish were feeding on the Tricos, they had seen enough of the natural pupae that they took my caddis imitation. It does not always work out this way, but keep in mind that it is sometimes more effective to show fish something a little different than what they are currently feeding on, especially if that something is a lot easier to see than the

Olive (top) and tan Graphic Caddis imitate emerging caddis larvae (called pupae). I most often fish these flies with a Leisenring Lift or swing them in front of feeding fish.

CHARLIE CRAVEN

naturals. I'll never forget the way the late day alpenglow reflected off those leaping rainbows.

Many of the caddis pupa patterns developed through the years have worked okay for me, but come up a little short on pressured fish requiring more accurate patterns that imitate the exact shape and size of the natural. In my mind many are too bulky, too large, too busy, and don't look like the real thing. Natural pupae have clean hydrodynamic lines. Their bodies are translucent and smooth with a distinct hump in the posterior. Their legs and antennae sweep back along the body and they have dark wing pads. They have no tails.

The name Graphic Caddis comes from the use of silver holographic Flashabou under the stretch-tubing body. The Flashabou gives the illusion of the silvery air bubble that accompanies a pupa as it ascends in the water column.

I fish the pattern in a variety of ways. During a caddis hatch, I often swing it into a riseform. I cast 6 to 8 feet above the trout, and raise the rod tip so the line is tight to the fly. I cast past the riseform so that when the fly swings into the fish it is right in its face. I drop the rod tip three or so feet above the fish to put some slack into the line, allowing the pattern to sink. Just before the fly gets to the fish I slowly raise the rod tip to imitate an ascending pupa. The technique was devised by Jim Leisenring over fifty years ago and is referred to as the Leisenring Lift. It can be a deadly approach.

Another effective presentation is to trail a Graphic Caddis off the bend of an adult pattern. Since caddis pupae drift before they hatch, a dead drift can work well, or giving a few twitches may trigger a take. Try both dead drifts and twitches and let the trout tell you which presentation is best. You can also swing an adult and caddis pupa dropper if there is no hatch in progress, but there has been a lot of caddis activity.

The Graphic Caddis is one of my favorite third flies when fishing a Hopper-Copper-Dropper. It is also an excellent choice as a second or third fly when nymph-fishing. I usually use 4 or 5X tippet when fishing pupas.

I think the size and shape of the pupa is the most important feature of a caddis, and the color just needs to be fairly close. With around 1,400 species, there is a wide range of colors, but if your pattern is the right size to imitate the naturals that the trout are feeding on, tan or olive will work in most cases. Of course there are exceptions, but it's impossible to carry countless different caddis pupae. A general rule of thumb I follow is to fish the

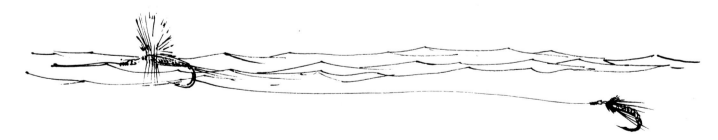

I often fish a Graphic Caddis under a Vis-A-Dun or an adult caddis. Not only do I fish this combination dead-drift, but I'll also let the flies swing at the end of the drift. The swinging Graphic Caddis often gets strikes from fish. During caddis hatches, I often swing the fly into a riseform. I cast 6 to 8 feet above the trout and past the riseform, so that by the time the fly swings it is in front of the fish.

olive pattern in the spring and early summer and tan in the late summer and fall. There is some overlap and there are exceptions, so this seasonal color pattern is not etched in stone. Usually the darker adult caddis, like the dark gray and dark brown colors, have olive pupae and the lighter tan caddis have tan pupae.

"The Graphic Caddis is my go-to pattern during a caddis hatch. I like to trail it behind a caddis dry and quarter it downstream so that it swings into a riseform. From spring through fall, I have used the Graphic Caddis on rivers throughout the Rocky Mountains, both during a hatch, and as a nymph. It works everywhere!"

—Jonathan Wexler, Playing Field
Promotions, Denver, Colorado

Every fly box should contain a selection of caddis pupae. I carry a good supply of tan and olive colors in sizes 14–18 and a few 20s. This will cover most, but not all situations. You can never cover every possible scenario. If you fish familiar waters, you know what you are going to encounter. If you are going to fish somewhere you are unfamiliar with, research whether you will need something else; for example, the October caddis is large and you will need some big pupae imitations.

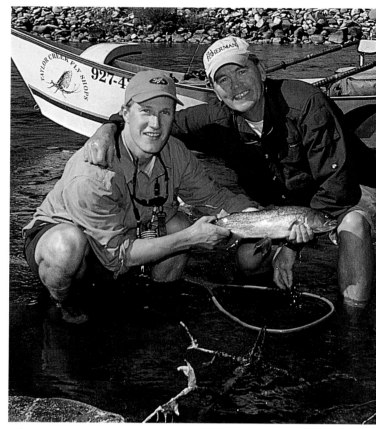

This nice cuttbow took a Graphic Caddis fished on the swing.
ROSS PURNELL

GRAPHIC CADDIS

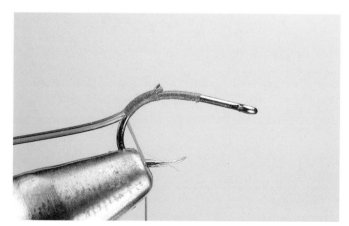

1. Insert the hook into the vise. Start the thread just in front of the halfway point on the shank. Wrap back to the start of the hook bend. Tie in a length of stretch tubing just behind the hook point. Wrap back over the tubing to about halfway down the bend of the hook. Leave the thread hanging at the farthest point back on the hook.

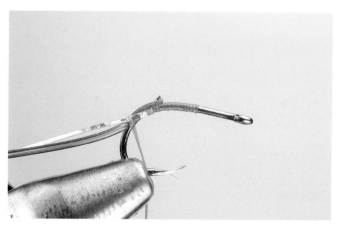

2. Tie in a single strand of silver holographic Flashabou at the bend of the hook.

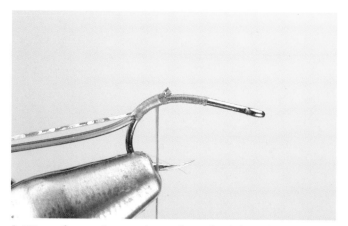

3. Wrap forward over the stub end of the Flashabou up to just behind the point on the hook.

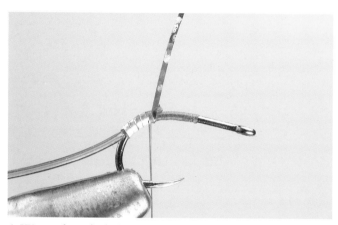

4. Wrap the Flashabou forward about three turns with tight, touching wraps. Tie the Flashabou off and clip the excess.

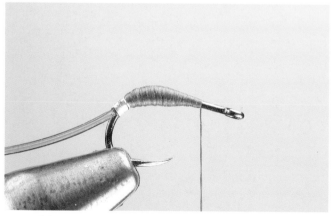

5. Build a reverse taper with the tying thread from the front edge of the Flashabou up to about two eye lengths back from the hook eye. The body should be fatter at the back than it is at the front, as shown here.

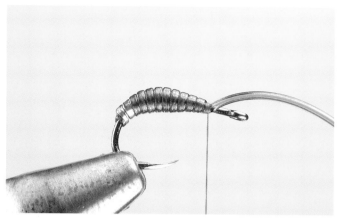

6. Wrap the stretch tubing forward over the thread underbody and Flashabou in tight touching turns. Tie the tubing off at the front of the thread taper with two tight turns of thread.

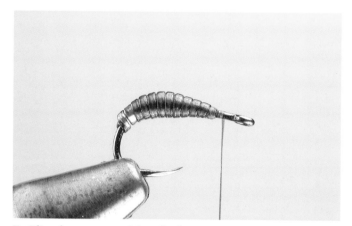

7. Clip the excess tubing flush.

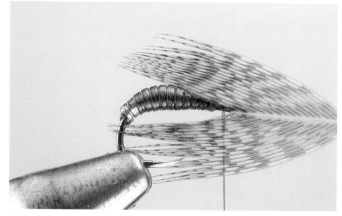

8. Select a brown Hungarian partridge feather and clip the center quill in the upper part of the feather, leaving the V-shaped feather shown here.

9. Lay the feather over the top of the hook with the out-side of the feather facing up. The point of the V should be against the hook shank at the front of the body and the tips of the fibers should extend back to the hook bend.

10. Grab the tips of the feather in your material hand and pinch them against the hook. Make two loose wraps of thread around the feather at the front of the body.

11. Release the tips of the feather from your grasp as you tighten the thread turns, allowing the fibers to splay around the hook shank. You may need to make a couple more wraps of thread to "walk" the fibers all the way around the hook.

12. Clip the butt ends from the partridge feather. Make a few turns of thread to form a smooth base for the ostrich herl head to follow.

13. Select a single herl from a natural gray ostrich feather. Tie this feather in by its butt end, with the inside of the feather facing forward, at the front edge of the hackle/body junction.

14. Lift the ostrich feather up and, with wet fingers, stroke the fibers back toward the hook bend. Folding the ostrich in this way will allow it to lie back along the shank.

15. Wrap the ostrich herl forward, one turn in front of the last, and sweep the fibers back after each turn. Tie the ostrich off at the hook eye and clip the excess.

16. Brush out the ostrich herl a bit with your fingertips to dry it and it should lie back along the fly as shown.

17. Tan Graphic Caddis, wet.

PATTERN VARIATION

CHARLIE CRAVEN

GRAPHIC CADDIS
(Tan)

Hook:	Size 14–16 Tiemco 2499SP-BL
Thread:	Tan 6/0 Danville
Abdomen:	Tan Wapsi stretch tubing
Tag:	Silver holographic Flashabou
Legs:	Brown Hungarian partridge body feather fibers
Head:	Natural gray ostrich

CHAPTER 10

Barr Emerger

I created the Barr Emerger in 1975 after a frustrating day fishing a Pale Morning Dun (PMD) hatch on Nelson's Spring Creek in Paradise Valley outside Livingston, Montana. There was a great hatch, and it seemed like every fish in the creek was rising to them. I was frustrated because not only was the Light Cahill I was fishing catching nothing, but also the trout were not even taking the real duns. They were eating little yellow specks off of the surface. I was baffled. I saw a trout "accidentally" eat a real dun, which it promptly spit out. I had no idea what was going on. It was obvious that these trout had eaten duns that had hooks in them and had learned to avoid eating things floating high on the water's surface.

Out of frustration, I put on an unweighted nymph and caught a nice rainbow. It was a male with a big mouth, and after landing, the fish kept his mouth wide open. I noticed many nymph shucks with partially emerged PMD adults stuck to the rakers on the base of his tongue. The PMDs were obviously hatching in the surface film, and the trout were picking off the helpless partially emerged PMDs. At my vise that night I created the PMD Emerger. The next day I went back to Nelson's and hooked every fish that I made a good presentation to. I was ecstatic.

The following spring I revisited the Paradise Valley spring creeks with a box full of a *Baetis* (BWO or Blue-Winged Olive) version of the emerger. I fished some good *Baetis* hatches and had the same success with the *Baetis* version as the PMD version the previous summer.

Thirty years ago, I fished nothing but dry flies to rising fish, but the Emerger changed the way I presented to rising fish on any river from those days on the spring creeks to the present. Having an emerger pattern during a hatch became a vital component when I was fishing to rising trout, especially pressured fish.

"We have sold the deadly Barr Emerger here in our shop for the past twenty-five years. This has been a terrific emerger pattern anywhere I fish PMD or *Baetis* hatches, but especially here on our Livingston Spring Creeks. This two-tone emerger

CHARLIE CRAVEN

PMD BARR EMERGER, DRY

Hook:	Size 16–22 Tiemco 101
Thread:	Light cahill 8/0 Uni-Thread
Tail:	Brown spade hackle fibers
Abdomen:	Blended olive brown dubbing
Wing case:	Pale olive or cream hackle fibers
Thorax:	PMD Superfine dubbing

was one of the first to imitate a helpless mayfly emerging from its nymphal shuck, and often the big fish really key in on the emergers in this stage. Once they are fully out of their shucks, with their upright wings, the fish seem to sense that these mayflies can fly off the water in an instant, while the emergers are sitting ducks."

—GEORGE ANDERSON, Yellowstone Angler, Livingston, Montana

The Barr Emerger was originally created to represent an emerging mayfly dun. Most mayflies have a one-year life cycle, and when the nymphs are mature they swim to the surface to emerge as adults. Some mayfly nymphs split their exoskeleton (shuck) before they reach the surface, which may explain why the old classic wet

Over the years I have added a lot of bells and whistles to the Barr Emerger, and all of the variations have performed well for me in various circumstances. However, pressured fish, especially large, pressured fish, often are conditioned to flash materials and beads, and the plain Barr Emerger still works best. LANDON MAYER

flies can be effective. The adult mayfly then feebly swims to the surface. The wet flies probably look like ascending adults. Other mayflies don't hatch until the nymph reaches the surface, whereupon the nymph starts splitting its exoskeleton. The exoskeleton of the mature nymph starts splitting open from the front portion of the nymph, and the adult wriggles free and floats along on the surface until the wings are dry enough to allow the adult to fly off.

The original version was tied on a dry-fly hook and was strictly fished on the surface film to rising trout. Years later, I am not sure when, I decided to try a sinking version tied on a curved hook. It proved to be effective fished as a nymph when there was no hatch.

Before beads and flash materials were common, I fished the pattern plain, but after seeing these materials, I quickly added them to the original emerger. A flashback and a bead version were a natural progression for the sunk pattern. All three styles are effective, although I

fish the Flashback Emerger most often because I have the most confidence in it. Some extremely pressured trout don't like the flash of a bead or flashback, so the plain version still has its place in the box. I know some guides who fish nothing but the bead version with great success. It comes down to what you have confidence in.

I was fishing with my friend Paul Russell who owns a guide service in Steamboat, Colorado. We were fishing to rising trout during a *Baetis* hatch on the Yampa River below Stagecoach Reservoir, an area that receives a lot of pressure. The trout would not eat duns, floating emergers, sunk flashback, or beadhead emergers. When I put the plain sunk version on I started hooking fish. Let the fish tell you what they want. In many instances, I have caught plenty of heavily pressured fish with the flashback.

One of the great attributes of the Barr Emerger is that trout don't seem to get conditioned to it. By conditioned I mean that after a trout has been caught on a fly imitating a particular insect, they tend to not want to eat that fly again. On several occasions I have caught the same trout more than once on the pattern during a hatch. I caught the same rainbow that was rising off the end of a log in Nelson's Spring Creek twice during a *Baetis* hatch. On the Green River in Utah, I caught a cutthroat three times that was rising off the end of a log during a PMD hatch. I knew they were the same fish because the light was good and after releasing the trout, I could see the fish swim back to the log and resume feeding. The pattern continues to produce to this day, despite its popularity and widespread use. Some patterns that fish get used to seeing lose their effectiveness after a while, but not this emerger pattern.

Another good attribute of the fly is that it serves double duty as both an imitation of an emerging mayfly

and an imitation of a stuck-in-the-shuck cripple. If a mayfly doesn't successfully escape its shuck it is called a cripple, and helplessly floats down the river, often into the open mouth of a trout. The floating version makes a perfect pattern to imitate these cripples.

The *Baetis* version of the emerger has over the years proven to be an effective winter pattern in the tailwaters of Colorado. It is one of the guides' favorite patterns. There was a photo of a 23-pound rainbow in *Fly Fisherman* several years ago caught by Brian Byerly on a size 20 *Baetis* Barr Emerger in the winter on the Taylor River. It is an effective pattern when the only active insects are midges, and it is one of my go-to patterns twelve months of the year. It catches fish year-round just about anywhere, and its productivity has not regressed.

DRY DROPPER

For years I had only fished one fly, whether fishing dry flies, nymphs, emergers, or streamers. When I first developed this pattern, I would fish the floating version to rising fish. This pattern, fished alone, caught lots of fish, but unless the light was just right and you could see the pattern well, it was difficult to judge if you were getting a drag-free drift—which you usually want—and it was difficult to see the fly, especially the darker *Baetis* pattern.

I had been fishing the Vis-A-Dun to represent adult mayflies since the late 1970s, but until that day with Jackson that I mentioned in the preface, fishing the Hopper-Dropper, I had never thought to hang an emerger off the hook bend of the dun. I decided to try dropping the emerger off the hook bend of the dry. That day was a huge breakthrough for fishing emergers to rising trout. I had always

fished the dry emerger in the surface film by itself, which often meant guess striking because it was difficult to see the pattern unless the light was perfect. The Vis-A-Dun was easy to see, let you know if you were getting a good and accurate drift, and acted as a strike indicator if the trout took the trailing emerger. During a hatch, trout feed on both emergers and duns, and some individual fish concentrate on one or the other. You have both bases covered by giving the fish a choice. I began catching a lot more fish when I started fishing a dry fly and an emerger together.

When fishing to rising trout during a hatch I start off with an appropriate Vis-A-Dun and floating emerger. If that is ineffective I put on the sunk version, most often the flashback. I let the trout tell me what they want.

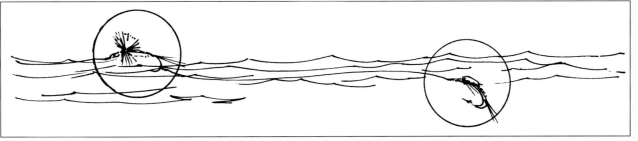

When I first developed the Barr Emerger, I would fish the floating version to rising fish—and just use the one fly. Now I often fish it with a Vis-A-Dun. The Vis-A-Dun is easy to see, lets me know if I am getting the right drift, and acts as a strike indicator. Plus, during a hatch, trout often feed on both emergers and duns, so the two flies cover both bases.

In my earlier life, I fished nothing but dry flies to rising fish, but the emerger changed the way I fished to rising fish on any river from those days on the spring creeks thirty years ago to the present. The importance of an emerger pattern during a hatch became a vital component when fishing to rising trout, especially pressured fish. LANDON MAYER

Most of the emerger patterns I carry imitate PMDs and *Baetis,* because those are the hatches I am most likely to encounter; however, by changing the color of the front part of the fly (which imitates the emerging adult), the Barr Emerger can be effective for any mayfly hatch you may encounter. For instance, a yellowish orange emerging portion would work well for eastern sulphurs.

When nymph fishing or fishing a Hopper-Copper-Dropper setup, the sunken version of the pattern is one of my most often-used bottom flies.

"If I had only one fly to fish spring through fall, without question, it would be a Barr Emerger: either the PMD or the BWO, depending on the predominant insect activity. This has been one of the most effective patterns that I have fished over the years. With a realistic profile and the perfect color combination, the trout will rarely turn it down. I believe the true test of a fly pattern is its effectiveness on the water and its longevity in the fly shops. Year in and year out, the Barr Emerger is in high demand by the fly shops and anglers throughout the world: it simply works. I look forward to future fishing and guide trips using this fly and the smiles of success that I know will follow."

—LANDON MAYER, Colorado Springs, Colorado

PMD BARR EMERGER, DRY

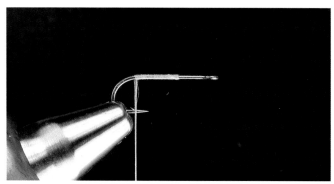

1. Insert the hook into the vise. Start the thread at the 80 percent point on the shank and wrap a smooth thread base back to the hook bend.

HOOK SIZE	BEAD
16	3/32 inch
18	5/64 inch
20–22	1/16 inch

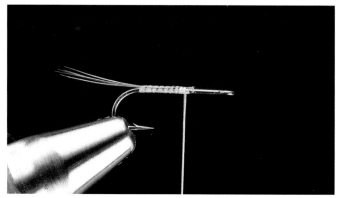

2. Tie in a dozen brown hackle fibers at the bend. Take care not to flare the tailing fibers. Wrap forward over the butt ends of the hackle fibers to the 80 percent point and cut the excess off at that point.

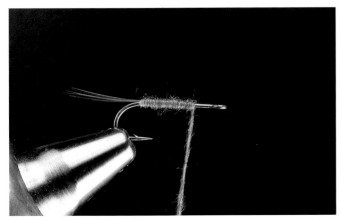

3. Dub the thread and start building the abdomen from the base of the tail to the 80 percent point. Keep the abdomen thin.

4. Fatten the front end of the abdomen up just slightly. Wrap the bare thread back over the front edge of the abdomen to the 75 percent point.

5. Select a cream or pale olive hackle feather for the wing case. Strip a dozen fibers from one side of the feather and try to keep the tips aligned.

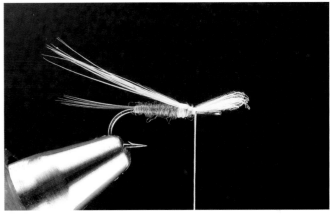

6. Tie this clump of hackle fibers in at the 75 percent point.

7. Wrap forward over the stub ends to secure them and clip the excess.

8. Dub the thorax from the front of the hook back up to the base of the wing case.

9. Return the dubbed thread to about one eye length back from the hook eye. You should have a round thorax as shown here.

12. Pull the other half of the hackle fibers back along the near side of the hook and bind them in place as you did the first clump.

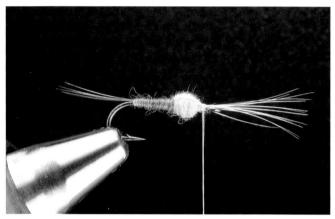

10. Pull the wing case over the top of the thorax and tie the hackle fibers down behind the hook eye.

13. Build a smooth thread head and whip-finish. Clip the thread.

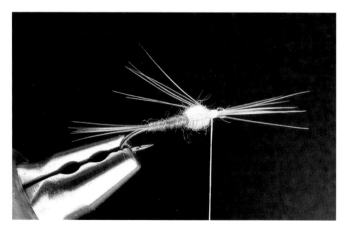

11. Divide the remaining butt ends of the wing case hackle fibers and pull half back along the far side of the hook. Bind these fibers in place with a few tight turns of thread.

14. Clip the legs so they extend to the back of the wing case. Clip the tail so it is about one-half a shank length long.

PMD Barr Emergers. From left to right: Barr Emerger (dry), Beadhead Flashback Barr Emerger, Beadhead Barr Emerger, Flashback Barr Emerger, and Barr Emerger (wet). CHARLIE CRAVEN

PATTERN VARIATIONS

PMD BARR EMERGER, WET

Hook:	Size 16–22 Tiemco 2487
Thread:	Light cahill 8/0 Uni-Thread
Tail:	Brown spade hackle fibers
Abdomen:	Blended olive and brown dubbing
Wing case:	Pale olive or cream hackle fibers
Thorax:	PMD Superfine dubbing

PMD FLASHBACK BARR EMERGER

Hook:	Size 16–22 Tiemco 2487
Thread:	Light cahill 8/0 Uni-Thread
Tail:	Brown spade hackle fibers
Abdomen:	Blended olive and brown dubbing
Flashback:	Mirage tinsel (medium)
Wing case:	Pale olive or cream hackle fibers
Thorax:	PMD Superfine dubbing

PMD BEADHEAD BARR EMERGER

Hook:	16–22 Tiemco 2487
Bead:	Brass (see chart)
Thread:	Light cahill 8/0 Uni-Thread
Tail:	Brown spade hackle fibers
Abdomen:	Blended olive and brown dubbing
Wing case:	Pale olive or cream hackle fibers
Thorax:	PMD Superfine dubbing

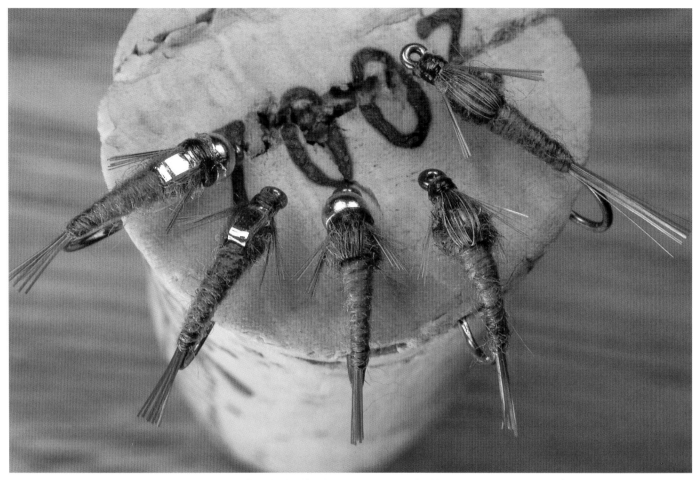

BWO Barr Emergers. From left to right: Beadhead Flashback Barr Emerger, Flashback Barr Emerger, Beadhead Barr Emerger, Barr Emerger (wet), Barr Emerger (dry). CHARLIE CRAVEN

BWO FLASHBACK BARR EMERGER

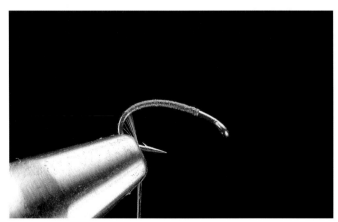

1. Insert the hook into the vise. Start the thread two eye lengths back from the hook eye and wrap a smooth thread base about halfway down the bend of the hook.

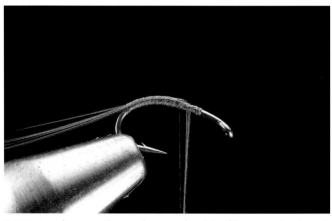

2. Tie in about a dozen brown hackle fibers at the bend. Wrap forward over the butt ends to the midpoint on the shank. Clip the butt ends of the hackle fibers close to the hook. Do not worry about the length of the tail at this point, as it will be clipped to length later.

3. Dub a tapered abdomen with the olive brown dubbing from the base of the tail up to about one eye length back from the hook eye. Wrap the thread back over the front edge of the dubbing to just in front of the hook point as shown.

4. Tie in a single strand of Mirage flash along the top of the abdomen. Wrap back over the flash to about one-third of the way back from the hook eye.

5. Tie in a clump of about a dozen blue dun hackle fibers by their butt ends at the base of the flash. Clip any excess butt ends from the hook. Note the bare space at the front of the hook.

CHARLIE CRAVEN

BWO FLASHBACK BARR EMERGER

Hook:	Size 16–24 Tiemco 2487
Thread:	Iron gray 8/0 Uni-Thread
Tail:	Brown hackle fibers
Abdomen:	Blended olive and brown dubbing
Flashback:	Mirage tinsel (medium)
Wing case/Legs:	Blue dun hackle fibers
Thorax:	Adams gray Superfine dubbing

6. Dub a small round thorax with the Adams gray Superfine dubbing. Be sure to reserve about an eye length of bare space (only thread) at the front of the hook.

7. Pull the blue dun hackle fibers over the top of the thorax and tie them down with two tight wraps of thread just behind the eye.

8. Pull the flash over the top of the hackle fiber wing case and tie it down behind the eye as well.

9. Pull the long end of the flash back over the hook and tie it down again with two more tight wraps of thread. Folding the flashback in this manner prevents it from pulling out while fishing.

10. Divide the tips of the hackle fiber wing case into two even bunches. Pull the first bunch back along the far side of the hook and bind them in place. The legs should be parallel to the thorax along the side of the hook.

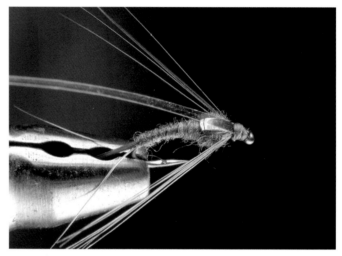

11. Pull the other half of the hackle fibers back along the near side of the hook and bind them in place as you did with the first clump.

12. Clip the remaining flash flush against the front of the thorax. Clip the hackle fibers so they are just a bit longer than the thorax and finally, clip the tail fibers so they are about one-half the shank length long.

PATTERN VARIATIONS

BWO BARR EMERGER, DRY

Hook:	Size 16–24 Tiemco 101
Thread:	Iron gray 8/0 Uni-Thread
Tail:	Brown hackle fibers
Abdomen:	Blended olive and brown dubbing
Wing case/Legs:	Blue dun hackle fibers
Thorax:	Adams gray Superfine dubbing

BWO BARR EMERGER, WET

Hook:	Size 16–24 Tiemco 2487
Thread:	Iron gray 8/0 Uni-Thread
Tail:	Brown hackle fibers
Abdomen:	Blended olive and brown dubbing
Wing case/Legs:	Blue dun hackle fibers
Thorax:	Adams gray Superfine dubbing

BWO BEADHEAD BARR EMERGER

Hook:	Size 16–24 Tiemco 2487
Bead:	Brass (see chart)
Thread:	Iron Gray 8/0 Uni-Thread
Tail:	Brown hackle fibers
Abdomen:	Blended olive and brown dubbing
Wing case/Legs:	Blue dun hackle fibers
Thorax:	Adams gray Superfine dubbing

CHAPTER 11

Micro Emerger

The Micro Emerger is a slim, miniature version of the original Barr Emerger designed to imitate tiny mayfly emergers and nymphs. The brown and dun color fishes well as a tiny *Baetis* emerger or as a midge pupa. The black color also imitates a tiny *Baetis* nymph, many of which are dark, almost black, and slim.

I fish the Micro Emerger under an indicator as the last fly in a series of nymphs or drop it off the bend of a Vis-A-Dun during a mayfly or midge hatch. If small *Baetis* are hatching, I usually drop the micro *Baetis* emerger off the bend of an appropriately sized *Baetis* Vis-A-Dun. If midges are hatching, I drop a *Baetis* or black Micro Emerger off the bend of a Trico Vis-A-Dun.

As the season progresses, the *Baetis* get smaller, and by September, they are usually a size 22 and smaller. The Micro Emerger comes in handy to imitate these small insects and I always make sure they are in my box in the fall and winter.

CHARLIE CRAVEN

MICRO EMERGER
(Rusty Brown)

Hook:	Size 18–24 Tiemco 101
Thread:	Rusty brown 6/0 Danville
Tail:	Brown hackle fibers
Abdomen:	Tying thread
Wing case:	Dun hackle fibers
Thorax:	Adams gray Superfine dubbing
Legs:	Dun hackle fibers

The Micro Emerger in both black and rust and dun are standbys in my fly boxes. CHARLIE CRAVEN

I fish Micro Emergers most often in the fall and winter, when Baetis *and midges are the most common foods for trout.*
LANDON MAYER

MICRO EMERGER

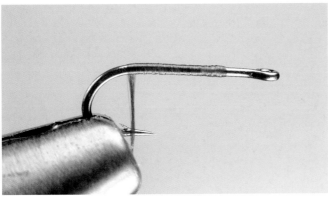

1. Insert the hook into the vise. Start the thread two eye lengths back from the hook eye and make a smooth thread base to the bend.

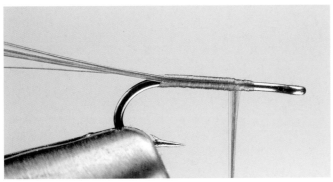

2. Tie in a small clump of brown hackle fibers at the bend for the tail. The length of these fibers is not important, as we will clip them to length later. Wrap the thread forward over the butt ends of the tailing fibers and clip them off at the 75 percent point. Make another layer of thread to build a slim abdomen from the base of the tail to the 75 percent point.

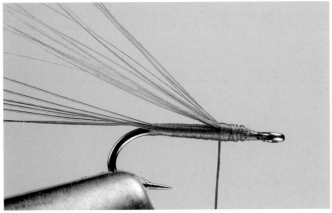

3. Strip about a dozen fibers from a blue dun neck hackle and tie them in by their butt ends at the 75 percent point on top of the hook shank.

4. Dub the thread with the Adams Superfine dubbing and build a small ball for the thorax. Be sure to leave a bare eye length of space between the hook eye and the front of the thorax dubbing.

5. Pull the gray hackle fibers tightly forward over the dubbed thorax and tie them down with two firm wraps behind the hook eye.

6. Divide the tips of the gray hackle fibers and pull half back along the far side of the thorax. Bind these fibers in place with one or two tight turns of thread. The legs should be in the same plane as the hook shank when viewed from the side.

7. Pull the other half of the remaining hackle fiber tips back along the near side of the hook and bind them in place as well.

8. Make a few turns of thread to smooth out the head, whip-finish and clip the thread. Trim the legs so they are just slightly longer than the wing case. Trim the tail fibers so they are about one-half the length of the hook shank.

9. Coat the abdomen and head with a thin layer of Sally Hansen's Hard As Nails.

PATTERN VARIATION

CHARLIE CRAVEN

MICRO EMERGER
(Black)

Hook:	Size 18–24 Tiemco 101
Thread:	Black 6/0 Danville
Tail:	Black hackle fibers
Abdomen:	Tying thread
Wing case:	Black hackle fibers
Thorax:	Black Superfine dubbing
Legs:	Black hackle fibers

Pure Midge Larva

When I was about ten years old I used to fish a little lake near my home in Seattle that I could bicycle to. I would fly-fish, but I had limited success. An old-timer was there all the time and was always catching fish. I would rake out a small fish on occasion, but he would hammer fish, with some nice ones on a regular basis. I was young and shy, but finally got up the nerve to ask him how he was catching all those fish. A very nice man, he gave me some flies and told me to retrieve them slowly. The patterns didn't look like much—just monofilament wrapped over a black thread underbody. I tied on his pattern and retrieved it slowly per his instruction. I started hooking fish, but struck a little too enthusiastically and broke off every fly he gave me. The monofilament tippet material was of very poor quality, so I will place all blame on the break-offs on the material, not my ineptness. It was an easy fly to tie, so I duplicated his pattern, and with a little better touch started landing fish in the lake on a regular basis. I had no idea what a midge larva or pupa was at the time, but looking back, I am sure that's what the trout were taking the pattern for. For years after that, I fished that monofilament and black thread pattern with success.

I had forgotten about it until one mid-January in the late 1990s. Jackson Streit, owner of Mountain Anglers fly shop in Breckenridge, Colorado, and I decided we needed to get out and catch a few fish, even though temperatures were well below freezing. We knew we would be dealing with iced-up guides, cold fingers, and inactive trout due to the cold water. My guess is when the water is really cold, a trout's metabolism is so depressed that one or two midge larvae a week might be all they eat. I am being facetious, but the colder the water temperature is, the lower a fish's metabolism is, and the less food they require.

Even in the dead of winter, the Colorado River near Parshall, Colorado, doesn't freeze for a couple of miles

The Pure Midge is a simple midge larva imitation that you can tie in a wide range of colors. As you can see, not all colors are imitative. Some of my best producers are blue and chartreuse.

CHARLIE CRAVEN

CHARLIE CRAVEN

PURE MIDGE LARVA
(Fluorescent Red)

Hook:	Size 16–24 Tiemco 2488 or 2488H
Thread:	Fluorescent red 70-denier Ultra Thread
Body:	Clear microtubing
Head:	Tying thread coated with Sally Hansen's Hard As Nails

Since midges are a critical food source for trout year-round, especially tailwater and stillwater trout, a Pure Midge dropped off the bend of a Copper John is a good choice when fishing waters where midges are important. LANDON MAYER

The warmer water of the Williams Fork (above) keeps the Colorado River ice-free in winter. ROSS PURNELL

downstream, from where the Williams Fork (a short tailwater that dumps relatively warm water into the river) enters it. Above the confluence, the Colorado River is covered in ice.

That day, midges were hatching but nothing but tiny trout sporadically rose. The Colorado, like most rivers, has an abundant population of midge larvae. Jackson told me that recently his best pattern on the Colorado had been a pale olive midge larva. He gave me some patterns, and we had steady action, considering the time of year: probably around four to five fish per hour. When our fingers got so cold they quit working, we called it a day.

That evening I remembered the old man's pattern and tied the first Pure Midge Larva to imitate the pale olive midge larvae. I used clear tubing over various colors of tying thread for the body. The tubing was easier to work with than mono, and it looked better. The tubing added segmentation as well as translucency. I finished off the pattern with a shiny black head built up a little larger than the body. Most midge larvae have a darker head contrasting with the body, but the red ones, also called bloodworms, are all red. I experimented with lots of different colors and for the red pattern I used the same color for the head as the body. I kept it for another cold-weather day at the river.

There are over 1,000 species of aquatic midges. They are found coast to coast in every type of flowing and still water. They are especially abundant in tailwaters below reservoirs. Midges undergo a complete metamorphosis—egg, larva, pupa, and adult. Whereas most aquatic insects have a one-year life cycle, midges can have up to four or five cycles in a year, depending on water temperatures in which they live. The warmer the water the more cycles they will have. Midge larvae can range in length from ¹⁄₁₆ to 4 inches; however, most of the midge larvae that are important to fly fishers are ⅛ to ½ inch long. Some stillwater larvae can be a size 14 or 12, but larvae in most rivers are size 18 and smaller.

Why are these tiny larvae such important food sources? Midge larvae drift at all hours of the day, and because they are so prolific, there can be massive numbers of individuals drifting in the currents at one time, providing an important, consistent food source for trout. Midge larvae can be present in staggering numbers, sometimes upward of 50,000 individuals per square meter. They are available to trout on a regular basis, and are familiar and readily accepted. Midge larvae are easily dislodged during rising water, making for an easy meal.

In the winter, midges are about the only aquatic insect that are active, and in many fisheries midge larvae make up a significant part of a trout's diet at this time.

Trout feed on midges all year, but in winter, they often feed exclusively on them. JOHN BARR

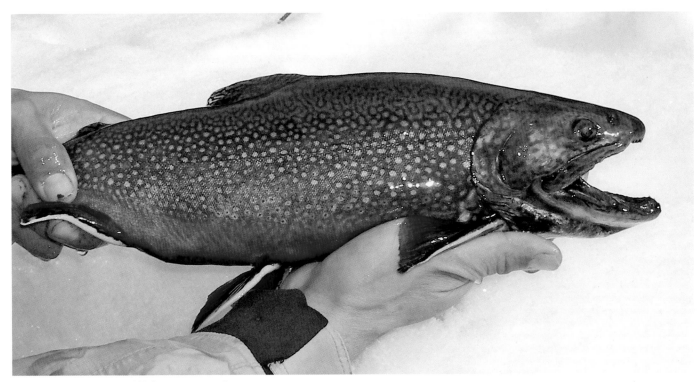

This large brook trout fell for a Pure Midge Larva. LANDON MAYER

Their sheer abundance can make them a primary source of nutrition year-round in some fisheries, and they can grow large trout. A prime example of this is the San Juan River outside of Farmington, New Mexico. I have heard that at least 50 percent of the trout's diet in the San Juan consists of midge larvae and pupae, and the river has a large population of big trout.

Midge larvae come in a wide variety of colors, from white to black. They are simple little worms, with a segmented body and often a darker head that contrasts with the body. The red larva, commonly called a bloodworm, has a red body and head. The Pure Midge Larva can be tied in a variety of colors. I tie the pattern in seven colors: black, blue, chartreuse, pale olive, tan, and fire red. One of these colors will usually work. I try to match the color of the midge larvae where I am fishing. Although I have never heard of a natural blue midge larva, blue can be an

effective color. I have found that the fire red can be more effective than a regular red. Chartreuse is a very effective color, perhaps because it can be taken for an immature or micro caddis larva.

I fish the pattern as the bottom fly in a two- or three-nymph setup in both rivers and lakes. In flowing waters I like to dead-drift the nymphs with an occasional twitch. The natural larvae will squirm and move around a little bit as they are drifting. In still waters I usually fish the larva under an indicator, also with some twitches. I tied the fly on a curved hook to suggest the profile of a midge larva drifting curled up in the current. While drifting in a river or ascending to the surface in still water, midge larvae will writhe and twist their bodies.

I guess you could say I knocked off the old man's pattern, but I bet if he is fishing some lake in the sky he would be happy that a version of his fly lives on.

PURE MIDGE LARVA

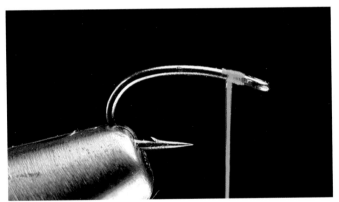

1. Insert the hook into the vise. Attach the thread behind the hook eye.

3. Clip the excess tubing from the front end of the fly, and return the thread to the hook eye. Keep the thread base smooth as you wrap forward.

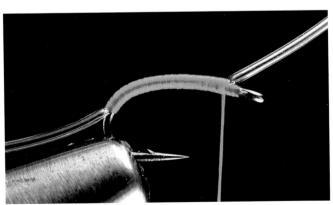

2. Tie in a length of microtubing right behind the hook eye. Stretch the tubing slightly as you wrap back over it to the bend.

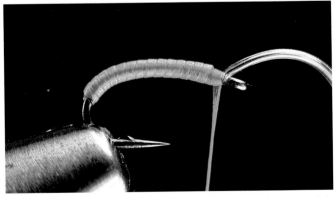

4. Wrap the tubing forward over the thread base with touching turns. Tie the tubing off just behind the eye of the hook.

5. Clip the excess tubing flush and build a smooth, round thread head. Whip-finish and clip the thread.

6. Coat the thread head with a layer of Sally Hansen's Hard As Nails.

PATTERN VARIATIONS

PURE MIDGE LARVA
(Fluorescent Green)

Hook:	Size 16–24 Tiemco 2488 or 2488H
Thread:	Fluorescent green 70-denier Ultra Thread
Body:	Clear microtubing
Head:	Black 8/0 Uni-Thread coated with Sally Hansen's Hard As Nails

PURE MIDGE LARVA
(Chartreuse)

Hook:	Size 16–24 Tiemco 2488 or 2488H
Thread:	Chartreuse 70-denier Ultra Thread
Body:	Clear microtubing
Head:	Black 8/0 Uni-Thread coated with Sally Hansen's Hard As Nails

PURE MIDGE LARVA
(Tan)

Hook:	Size 16–24 Tiemco 2488 or 2488H
Thread:	Tan 6/0 Danville
Body:	Clear microtubing
Head:	Black 8/0 Uni-Thread coated with Sally Hansen's Hard As Nails

PURE MIDGE LARVA
(Olive)

Hook:	Size 16–24 Tiemco 2488 or 2488H
Thread:	Olive 70-denier Ultra Thread
Body:	Clear microtubing
Head:	Black 8/0 Uni-Thread coated with Sally Hansen's Hard As Nails

PURE MIDGE LARVA
(Hot Orange)

Hook:	Size 16–24 Tiemco 2488 or 2488H
Thread:	Hot orange 70-denier Ultra Thread
Body:	Clear microtubing
Head:	Black 8/0 Uni-Thread coated with Sally Hansen's Hard As Nails

PURE MIDGE LARVA
(Red)

Hook:	Size 16–24 Tiemco 2488 or 2488H
Thread:	Red 70-denier Ultra Thread
Body:	Clear microtubing
Head:	Black 8/0 Uni-Thread coated with Sally Hansen's Hard As Nails

PURE MIDGE LARVA
(Blue)

Hook: Size 16–24 Tiemco 2488 or 2488H
Thread: Blue 6/0 Danville
Body: Clear microtubing
Head: Black 8/0 Uni-Thread coated with
             Sally Hansen's Hard As Nails

PURE MIDGE LARVA
(Black)

Hook: Size 16–24 Tiemco 2488 or 2488H
Thread: Black 70-denier Ultra Thread
Body: Clear microtubing
Head: Black 8/0 Uni-Thread coated with
             Sally Hansen's Hard As Nails

PURE MIDGE LARVA
(White)

Hook: Size 16–24 Tiemco 2488 or 2488H
Thread: White 70-denier Ultra Thread
Body: Clear microtubing
Head: Black 8/0 Uni-Thread coated with
             Sally Hansen's Hard As Nails

CHAPTER 13

Damselfly Nymph

My first experience fishing damselfly nymphs was at Henry's Lake in Idaho in the early 1970s. I researched the lake's hatches and knew that there would be some damsel activity when I planned to be there in early July. I arrived at the lake with a bunch of Polly Rosborough's damselfly nymphs. The pattern was fairly productive, and the experience hooked me for life on fishing still waters and fishing damselfly hatches. Polly's pattern was simple and consisted of an olive marabou tail, olive yarn body, and an olive wing case. I wanted the fly to look a little better to my eye, even though his pattern was effective. I added a dubbed body, burnt mono eyes, a mono ribbed, Ziploc-backed abdomen, and legs. Who knows if my pattern fished any better than Polly's, but it looked good and it worked.

In the years that followed my Henry's Lake experience, I sought out local waters that had damselfly hatches. Some of the most exciting trout fishing I have ever experienced was in July and August at Elevenmile Reservoir near Hartsel, Colorado, during the late 1970s through the early 1990s. Most stillwater fishing is blind fishing, either casting and retrieving or indicator fishing. At Elevenmile it was all wading and sight-casting to boils or head and tail rises. It was freshwater flats fishing at its finest. The rainbows, ranging from 3 to 9 pounds, were in 1 to 4 feet of water, and once hooked would run like bonefish off the flat into deeper water, and pull like yellowfin tuna.

One time I hooked a big rainbow and he took off on a blistering run. But there was a knot in the backing and it finally seized up, and the fish popped the tippet. I changed reels and still had a good morning of fishing. A few days later, I took my half-hitched reel to the fly shop and on a line-winding machine we measured 94 yards of backing to where the backing finally locked up.

These flats were loaded with northern pike up to 30 or more pounds, which liked to eat smaller trout, so there were only large fish. I would spend the night near the water in a tent, get up early, and have breakfast and

CHARLIE CRAVEN

DAMSELFLY NYMPH

Hook:	Size 10–14 Tiemco 200R
Thread:	Olive 6/0 Danville
Eyes:	Melted 12-pound-test Mason hard monofilament
Tail:	Olive marabou
Rib:	4X tippet material
Shellback:	Tan Thin Skin
Abdomen:	Light olive Wapsi Sow Scud dubbing
Legs:	Mallard flank dyed olive
Head/Thorax:	Light olive Wapsi Sow Scud dubbing

watch for that first boil of the day. The seagulls would show up and station themselves at the water's edge, and wait for the damselfly nymphs to crawl out of the water and pick them off. When I saw that first fish feed, usually around 8:00 A.M., my adrenalin was surging and I was ready to hit the water. I would start blind casting, all the while looking for rising fish.

If the fish's head and tail came out of the water when it rose, I could see the direction the fish was heading and had an idea of where to cast, but if all I could see

Damselfly migrations provide exciting opportunities to catch fish in the shallows. ROSS PURNELL

The Barr Damselfy Nymph is modeled after Polly Rosborough's pattern, but I added a few elements such as monofilament eyes and legs and a shellback. CHARLIE CRAVEN

was a boil, I just had to cast in the direction I thought the fish was heading and hope for a strike. I would strip slowly and occasionally mix in a hand-twist retrieve. On every cast my adrenalin surged because I could see boils and rises everywhere. The fish were cruising, so you had to have some luck to get your nymph in a position for the trout to see it. One of the great highs in fly fishing is getting tight, and when there is going to be a fifty yard or longer jump-filled run after getting tight, it is as good as it gets. When the hatch ended around midday, I would have lunch, regroup, and grab my 8-weight for an afternoon of pike fishing on the same flats. Those days wade-fishing the flats of Elevenmile Reservoir are some of my fondest memories of all my fishing.

Damselfy nymphs prefer to live in weed beds. When they mature, usually beginning in June or July, they migrate to shore, crawl out, shed their exoskeletons, and transform into adults. The best fishing with damselfy nymph patterns takes place when the nymphs migrate toward shore. The nymphs range in color from pale olive to brown, depending on the habitat that they live in. Many aquatic organisms take on the color of the habitat in which they live. I have found that color is not too critical, and that trout don't key in on a specific color, just the nymph itself. If your size is correct, and you fish the pattern in an appropriate manner, you will have success. Some people make the mistake of fishing a pattern that is too large. You are usually more successful with a smaller pattern—sizes 12 and 14 on a 3XL hook will usually work just fine.

An abundant damselfly nymph migration can cause the fish to go into a feeding frenzy. The slow-swimming nymphs are easy pickings for trout. Damselfly nymphs migrating toward the shore can cause some of the largest fish in the lake to go on a feeding binge. If the fish are feeding near the surface, you will see boils and head and tail rises. Sometimes damselfly nymphs do not make it to shore and climb out of the water on an aquatic plant that is sticking out of the water offshore, or sometimes onto your float tube or waders. Wherever they find something to crawl up on, they will do so, so it's a good idea to look for these areas.

Although in my experience the nymphs have been more important than the adults, I have heard of situations where the adults have triggered feeding. I have never been on the water when the adult was a factor, but I have heard some great stories about catching fish on the adults. Most of us are familiar with damselfly adults: they look like small dragonflies flitting around ponds, lakes, and slow-moving sections of rivers. The adults' slim bodies are often a shade of blue, but their color can range from pale green to tan. Damselflies are feeble fliers and a wind gust can land them in the water, which can make adult patterns important at times. Low-flying, egg-laying adults can generate some explosive top-water takes.

Some may confuse damselflies and dragonflies. Dragonflies are usually much larger and heavier bodied than damselflies, and are much faster and more powerful fliers. However, there are some small dragonflies. The easiest way to tell them apart is that, when at rest, the dragonflies hold their wings outstretched in a horizontal position, whereas damsels hold their wings back on top of their abdomen. The nymphs differ as well—dragonfly nymphs are thick and squat and damselfly nymphs are slender.

When fish are taking damsels in shallow water or near the surface, I usually fish a floating line and a 9-foot leader with 3X fluorocarbon tippet. The takes can be

Damselfly nymph. DAVE HUGHES

unexpected, and with the potential for a real heavyweight, stout tippet is a good idea. If there are damsels hatching, but no surface activity, and you are casting and retrieving, you will need an intermediate to fast-sinking line depending on the water depth. Rest assured, the trout are feeding on the nymphs if there is a hatch in progress. With the sinking lines, you can use a 4- to 5-foot leader with a 3X fluorocarbon tippet. My retrieve is usually a slow strip or a medium-speed hand twist.

For pressured fish, indicator fishing may be necessary to get consistent takes. When I am indicator fishing in still water, my setup is always the same. I use an indicator set so that the last fly is right above the bottom. During a damselfly hatch, my top fly is always a green or chartreuse Copper John to sink the flies. My next two flies are damselfly nymphs—the second a size 12, and the third a size 14. I use lighter tippet when indicator fishing because you do not have the surprise grabs, and you set with more control. I use 4X fluorocarbon to the Copper John, and either 4X or 5X for the next two flies, depending on the size of the fish and how much weed growth there is. I cast out and let all the flies sink. Keep alert while the flies are sinking, because you may get a take on the drop. After they have sunk, I will give a tiny slow hand twist, let it sit, and repeat until the indicator is back to the boat. When raising your flies be ready for a take.

DAMSELFLY NYMPH

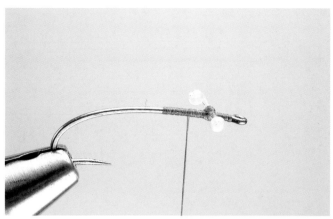

1. Insert the hook into the vise. Attach melted mono eyes to the hook shank with figure-eight wraps about three eye lengths back from the hook eye.

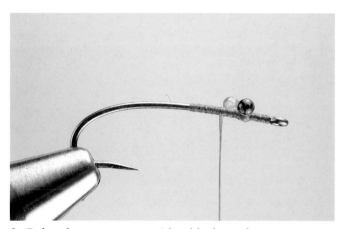

2. Color the mono eyes with a black marker.

3. Wrap the tying thread, forming a smooth thread base back to the bend of the hook. Tie in a small clump of olive marabou at the bend, forming the tail. The tail should be about a gap-width long.

4. Lift the butt ends of the marabou and wrap the thread forward to just behind the eyes. Tie the marabou down again at this point.

5. Clip the excess marabou and wrap the thread back to the base of the tail, binding down the marabou fibers as you go. Attaching the tail in this manner allows for a smooth, even underbody all the way up the hook.

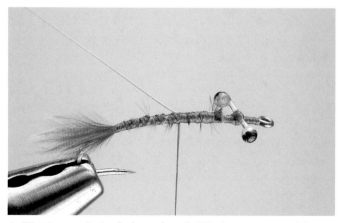

6. Tie in an 8-inch length of 4X tippet material just behind the eyes on the far side of the hook.

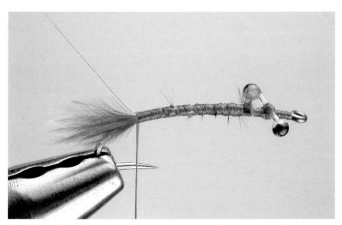

7. Wrap back over the mono to the base of the tail, keeping it along the far side of the hook shank.

8. Cut a tapered strip of Thin Skin that is, at its widest point, about half as wide as the hook gap.

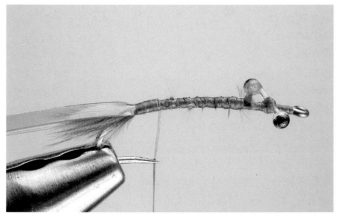

9. Remove the paper backing from the Thin Skin strip and tie the thin end in at the base of the tail.

10. Dub a thin abdomen about two-thirds of the way up the hook shank.

11. Tie in a small clump of dyed olive mallard flank along the far side of the hook shank immediately in front of the dubbed abdomen. The tips of the mallard should extend to the hook point.

12. Tie another clump in along the near side of the hook.

13. Clip the butt ends of the mallard fibers.

14. Dub from the front edge of the abdomen up to the hook eye, making figure-eight wraps through the eyes. The head and thorax should be slightly larger in diameter than the abdomen.

15. Pull the Thin Skin forward over the top of the fly and tie it down just behind the hook eye.

16. Rib the monofilament forward through the abdomen with tight, evenly spaced turns. When you get to the thorax area, make a single, wide turn of ribbing, dividing the head/thorax area in half just in front of the legs. Bring the remaining mono up to the hook eye by traveling across the bottom of the head. Tie the mono off at the hook eye.

17. Clip the mono and Thin Skin flush. Build a smooth thread head to cover the stubs and whip-finish the thread.

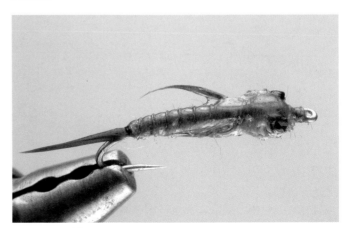

18. Damselfly, wet.

Vis-A-Dun

The Vis-A-Dun represents an adult mayfly, specifically the dun stage of an adult mayfly. I developed the original Vis-A-Dun about twenty-five years ago, but back then it was called the Bulletproof Dun, inspired by my search for a fly that was not only visible, but also durable. In subsequent years I started calling it the Vis-A-Dun because the name flowed off the tongue with less effort. Finding a dry-fly pattern that held up to several fish was a preoccupation of mine since all of the patterns I was using, especially the small ones, fell apart after a few trout. Flies size 18 and smaller, which I fish most frequently, require small hackles, which have thin, fragile stems. It was not unusual for trout's teeth—especially browns—to nick the thin hackle stems and have them unwind. My first prototypes had a hackle wrapped around the whole body in the traditional way, but the hackle stems broke frequently, which was an annoying problem. I resolved this issue by cutting the hackle fibers off under the body flush with the dubbing and then laid a bead of vinyl cement over the exposed hackle stem, cementing the stem to the dubbed body.

For improved visibility and durability I used a light-dun-colored polypropylene wing tied Comparadun style (fanned out from side to side). I tried wings tied with various other colors of poly for even better visibility, such as yellow and pink, but pressured fish, especially in flat water, usually refused those patterns. The fanned wing tended to lose its shape after a few fish, so I added a drop of vinyl cement to the base of the wing before or after fanning out the wing, which helped it keep its shape, even after catching many fish. After a dozen or more fish, the fly looks almost as good as when you tied it on. The hackle stem is not unbreakable, but you will probably lose the fly before it falls apart. The pattern is durable, but it doesn't prevent break-offs.

Baetis, PMDs, and Tricos constitute most of the mayfly activity in the Rocky Mountains (and the rest of the country, though PMDs are called Sulphurs in the East), which is where I fish most of the time. In fact, *Baetis,* Tricos, and PMDs are the big three insects on trout fisheries across the country and make up the longest and

CHARLIE CRAVEN

VIS-A-DUN
(*Baetis*)

Hook:	Size 18–24 Tiemco 101
Thread:	Iron gray 8/0 Uni-Thread
Tail:	Watery dun hackle fibers
Wing:	Light gray poly yarn
Abdomen:	Blue-Winged Olive Superfine dubbing
Hackle:	Light dun rooster
Thorax:	Blue-Winged Olive Superfine dubbing
Head:	Blue-Winged Olive Superfine dubbing
Adhesive:	Wapsi vinyl cement

most dependable mayfly hatches. Their hatches can last months, whereas many mayflies are unpredictable and may only hatch for a short period of time (like a week or two). Hatches that last for a while can result in some very picky trout. They may be easy to fool on duns in the early stages of the hatch, but as the hatch progresses be ready to hang an emerger off the bend of the dun. Pressured fish can get wise to dun patterns.

I load my fly boxes with patterns (in a variety of sizes) that imitate *Baetis,* PMDs, and Tricos. While these major insects are hatching on the streams that I fish, experience has taught me that I may also encounter

The Vis-A-Dun is the only mayfly dun imitation that I tie. I often use it to match the hatch, but I'll use it as the first of two flies when the second fly is hard to see. I caught this fish on a small Barr Emerger fishing in the film during a Baetis hatch, but it was the slight movement of the large, highly-visible Vis-A-Dun that told me to strike. LANDON MAYER

green drakes, red quills, or mahogany duns, so I carry some of those as well. On your home waters, you know what hatches you may encounter and will load your box accordingly.

The Vis-A-Dun pattern style can be adapted to any mayfly. If I am going to fish somewhere else in the country, I will research the hatches and conditions and add appropriate patterns. For example, if I were heading out East I would make some calls and find out what might be hatching where I was going to fish. If I was making an early spring trip, I'd also be sure to bring along some large size 12 Vis-A-Duns tied with gray bodies to imitate Quill Gordons or sizes 14 to 16 Vis-A-Duns tied with pinkish-gray bodies to imitate Hendricksons. The Vis-A-Dun is a generic pattern that is easily modified for any mayfly species. The Vis-A-Dun is also a passable spinner imitation, since it floats more or less in the film, and the hackle profile looks like spinner wings.

Size, specifically body length, profile, and presentation are the most important variables leading to successful fishing during a mayfly hatch. You may look at a mayfly dun floating by and think that it looks like a size 18. Then you pick one up and measure the body length of the natural against your fly: the natural has a size 22 body with large wings. If you are not sure what the body length of the natural is, pick one up with your hand or a small fine meshed screen. If the body length on your fly is the same length and size as the natural, the color of the body just needs to be close enough.

When I am fishing most mayfly hatches I usually start off with a dun tied to 6X and an emerger dropped off the bend with 6–10 inches of 6X. I will use either a Flashback Sunk Emerger or a plain floater in the film. I will let the trout tell me which emerger they want. For years all of my sunk emergers were plain, but I now most often fish a fly with flash. Some anglers swear by the bead version. Emerging mayflies often have a little glow, so the flashback or bead might imitate that. If the trout are keyed in on the duns, I will fish two duns sepa-

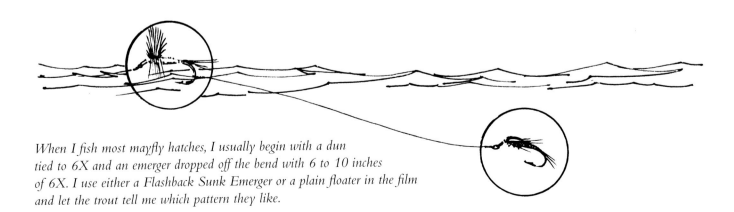

When I fish most mayfly hatches, I usually begin with a dun tied to 6X and an emerger dropped off the bend with 6 to 10 inches of 6X. I use either a Flashback Sunk Emerger or a plain floater in the film and let the trout tell me which pattern they like.

The Vis-A-Dun is a style of tying that you adapt for any mayfly. The colors that I usually tie are (from left to right) black, olive, yellow, and melon, but you can use dubbing to match local insects. CHARLIE CRAVEN

rated by around 10 inches of 6X tippet. I use a five-turn clinch knot to attach the flies and when tying the leader to the bend of the hook. When fishing the duns, you want a drag-free drift, but if you are fishing a Dun-Emerger combo a little twitch just before your flies get to the fish is okay, but a dead drift is usually your best bet.

I also fish the Vis-A-Dun as my lead fly when fishing a pattern that may be difficult to see, such as ants, beetles, or small caddis.

BAETIS

All across the country, *Baetis* are one of the most common hatches. I call all BWO-type insects *Baetis* even though some of them technically are not. *Baetis* is easier

to say, and people know what you are talking about. They range in size from 16 to 28. The hatches can be prolific in the spring and fall, especially on cloudy drizzly days, but they can be encountered any day from March through November. Most anglers don't consider *Baetis* as a summer hatch, but one day in July 2006 Van Rollo and I were fishing the Blue River near Silverthorne, Colorado, during one of the most intense *Baetis* hatches that either of has ever seen.

Even though *Baetis* can range in color from olive to brown/olive, I tie all my *Baetis* Vis-A-Duns with a medium-dark olive dubbing. If the body length is on the money, with a good presentation and an appropriate tippet and drag-free drift, it works just fine for any *Baetis* hatch that I have fished. If you are in the middle of a

If the trout are keyed in on the duns only, I fish two dun patterns separated by about 10 inches of 6X tippet.

Before I begin fishing dry-fly water, I usually start at the tailout of the pool (6) and spend a few minutes slowly and carefully scanning the water to mark where the fish are rising or likely spots such as seams, eddies behind rocks (5), foam or scum lines (2), and flats to deeper water (4). Do not overlook shallow water (1) or the water tight to the bank (3) where trout often hold. I then determine the best way to approach fish without spooking them. I stand below and to the side of a fish rising upstream, and then cast upstream so that my fly lands in the fish's feeding lane but, ideally, my leader does not.

good hatch, and have rising fish and are not doing well, it is usually a result of poor presentation (your casts aren't accurate or you are not getting a drag-free drift), your pattern is the wrong size (usually too large), the trout is seeing your leader (downsize and use fluorocarbon), or the trout are feeding on emergers (drop an emerger off the bend of your dun pattern).

"As a fly-fishing guide, the patterns I use day in and day out need to catch fish and be durable. The Vis-A-Dun is both. The superior visibility of the Vis-A-Dun makes it a surefire winner in my box.

Even on overcast days with tiny *Baetis* popping on the water, you can easily pick out the Vis-A-Dun. With the hackle being trimmed on the bottom, the pattern rides low and provides a perfect profile for the fish. The no-nonsense tying approach of the Vis-A-Dun can withstand the havoc that big trout wreak on a less durable fly. Heading out to the river without an arsenal of Vis-A-Duns in your fly box is like going to a strip club without dollar bills. You just won't get any attention."

—TRAPPER JOHN RUDD, owner and guide, Cutthroat Anglers, Silverthorne, Colorado

PALE MORNING DUNS

I call all mayflies with a pale olive, ginger, yellow, and sometimes melon-colored bodies Pale Morning Duns, even though they are all technically not PMDs. Also, even though they don't all hatch in the morning—some will hatch in the afternoon or evening—I still call them Pale Morning Duns, not Pale Evening Duns or Pale Afternoon Duns. Maybe my bug naming system would horrify an entomologist, but I'd like to think they make sense among other anglers.

PMDs are imitated on size 16–20 hooks and hatch from late spring through the summer, and in some waters, into the fall. They will hatch on both sunny and cloudy days. They are absolutely beautiful insects and the hatch is a favorite for many anglers, primarily because it lasts for a long time, the insects are relatively large (at least larger than Tricos and *Baetis*), and the fish key in on them.

PMDs have produced some of my fondest dry-fly fishing memories. I fished my first hatches on Nelson's and Armstrong Spring Creek in Montana's Paradise Valley more than thirty years ago. Over the years I have fished the hatch on numerous rivers, from the Henry's Fork of the Snake in Idaho to the South Platte and Colorado Rivers in Colorado. One of my most vivid memories involving PMDs occurred on the Colorado River, near Parshall, Colorado. I was fishing a large flat and there were lots of fish eating the duns. It was a nice hatch, but not spectacular. Then a thunderstorm rolled in and the lightning forced me to the bank. Suddenly the hatch increased tenfold. Right in front of me I watched hundreds of PMDs hatching, wriggling free of their shucks. Trout that had been casually sipping occasional mayflies went into a feeding frenzy. I watched in total disbelief. The lightning kept me out of the water, and I put my graphite rod (also known as a lightning rod) far away from my person. I had never seen a hatch that heavy and intense, and have not witnessed one since. It was a magical and surreal moment. After the storm passed, the hatch ended and so did the dry-fly fishing. There were no rising trout to be found.

TRICOS

Tricos are small mayflies ranging from size 18 to 28. They live in streams across the country and can hatch from late June through October. On some waters, I've heard that they can even hatch into November if the weather is mild. Once they start, hatches are dependable and last for months. Trico duns hatch late in the evening or most often very early in the morning, and usually the light is so poor you can barely see. The dun phase usually

I caught this fish on a PMD Vis-A-Dun during a hatch. Because of the fly's durable construction, one fly can last many nice fish and you don't waste precious time changing patterns.
JOHN BARR

does not provide good fishing due to the poor visibility, except in the late fall when the duns hatch during the morning. The spinners, once they die and are on the water's surface, can produce some incredible fishing. The warmer the day, the earlier the spinner fall occurs. I have seen spinners hit the water as early as 7 A.M. and as late as 11 A.M. On some rivers, the Trico spinner fall is a daily event for months and has produced some of my most memorable fishing to rising trout. Trico spinner falls can consistently bring up numerous trout and often some of the larger fish in the river.

The Trico Vis-A-Dun has a black body even though many adults have olive bodies and look like little *Baetis*. It was designed to be used during a Trico spinner fall with a drowned Trico spinner (see chapter 17). The dun serves as a strike indicator and lets you know if you are getting a drag-free drift, which is absolutely essential when fishing a Trico spinner fall. Remember, you are imitating dead insects, which do not move.

About 25 percent of the fish do take the dun. I think they key in on the black body, and probably at the right angle it gives the illusion of a spinner. For years I fished a single floating spinner, but it was frustrating and difficult fishing. For years I fished a black-bodied spinner with poly wings. I could always catch some fish but the fishing was tough. Trico spinner falls can be heavy, and competition from the naturals results in a pretty low chance that the trout will pick your fly out of all the naturals.

Trico swarms on the Yampa forecast an exciting morning of fishing Trico spinners. I use the black Vis-A-Dun as a Trico spinner imitation. LANDON MAYER

Since I went to the Trico, Vis-A-Dun, and drowned Trico combo, I usually fight fish during the spinner fall instead of making countless fruitless casts for every hook up.

In early 2000, I was fishing the Missouri River in Montana with my good friend George Anderson, owner of Yellowstone Angler in Livingston, Montana. George is the best dry-fly fisherman I have ever fished with. If he misses his target by an inch he considers it a bad cast. If he finds a rising trout, he usually hooks it.

We were fishing a Trico spinner fall one morning, and many fish were rising in the river. Trout will often pod up when feeding on Trico spinners, and we each found a pod. George was downstream from me about seventy-five yards, so I couldn't see him very well. I was fishing a Trico Vis-A-Dun and a drowned Trico spinner dropper. For about an hour I was almost constantly hooked up until there was a huge splash, like an explosion in the middle of the pod. George had snuck up behind me and had thrown a big rock in the river right were I was casting. I turned around, and George with a sly grin on his face informed me that I was cheating. He said that if I was not fishing with a single spinner I was breaking the rules of proper etiquette when fishing a spinner fall. He was just kidding. He then returned to his pod, and my pod resumed feeding farther up river, which George knew they would. When trout get into a feeding frenzy on a dense Trico spinner fall, you may put them down for a short while with a launched rock, but with all of those thousands of spinners floating down, they couldn't help but resume their feeding.

One of the most predictable and commonly-fished spinner falls is that of the Tricorythodes mayfly. Trico spinner falls occur in flowing waters throughout the country. The spinner is a small, size 18–28 mayfly with a stubby body. The bodies of the males are completely black, whereas the females have a black thorax and a mostly light olive abdomen. The lighter color is where the eggs were stored. I have heard that in some fisheries some trout will key in on the females, but I have always used just an all-black pattern and have not had problems in the places that I fish. Like all spinners, Tricos have clear wings.

Tricos can start hatching sometime in June and last into October. On some rivers there is a spinner fall almost every morning if the wind doesn't blow them away while they are in their mating swarm above the water. At times the number of spinners in the mating swarms can be staggering. The air can look like it is filled with steam or in the distance they can appear to be a white dust devil. The spinner fall can be dense, and the fish can get into a feeding frenzy, rising every couple of seconds. The spinner fall can bring some of the larger fish in the river to the top.

I encountered an interesting match the hatch situation on the Yampa River outside of Steamboat Springs, Colorado. The Trico spinner fall had concluded, but some fish continued to rise with no insects on the water. We finally caught one, and out of frustration pumped its stomach. Trico duns molt into spinners while in the air, and do so soon after hatching. The shed skin often ends up on the water's surface. These fish had been feeding on the shed skins of the Trico duns. That was the only time I had ever witnessed such an event.

VIS-A-DUN (BAETIS)

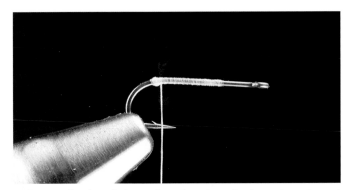

1. Insert the hook into the vise. Attach the tying thread at the 75 percent point and wrap a thread base back to the bend. Once at the bend, build a few wraps of thread into a small ball at the point directly above the point on the barb of the hook. This ball will help to splay the tails in the next steps.

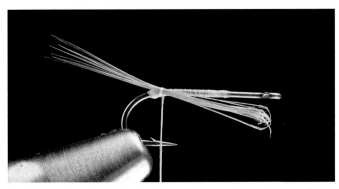

2. Select 6 or 8 spade hackle fibers and peel them from the quill, being careful to keep the tips even. Place the hackle fibers on the hook so the tips extend beyond the bend of the hook about one shank length. Bind the hackle fibers to the top of the shank with a couple turns of thread just in front of the thread ball.

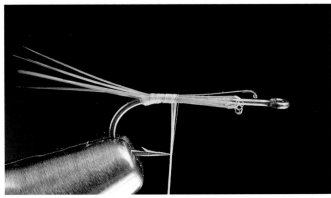

3. Wrap the tying thread back over the tailing fibers right up to the base of the thread ball. As you wrap, the fibers will splay out across the ball, forming a fan-shaped tail.

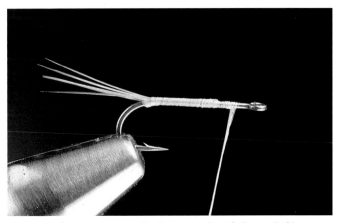

4. Wrap forward over the butt ends of the tail fibers to the midpoint on the hook and clip the excess.

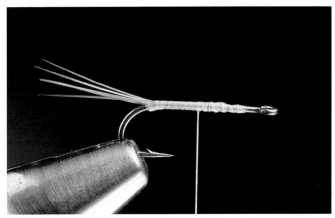

5. Wrap the thread forward to just behind the hook eye and then return it to the 50 percent point on the shank.

6. Clip and brush out a clump of poly yarn. About half the strand that comes off the card is about right for a size 16. Tie this clump in on top of the hook at the 60 per-cent point.

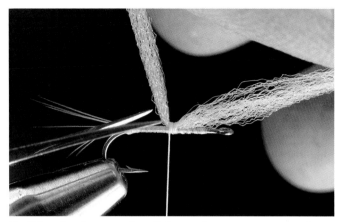

7. Clip the butt ends of the poly yarn at an angle as shown.

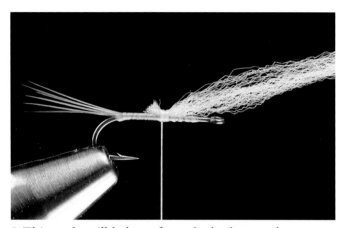

8. This angle will help to form the body taper later.

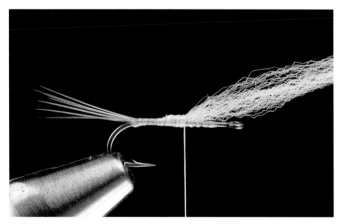

9. Wrap a smooth thread base over the butt ends, tapering up to the back of the wing as shown.

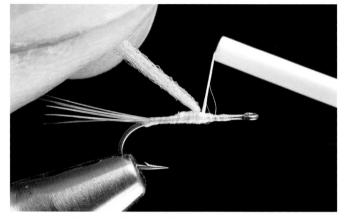

10. Bring the thread to the front of the wing.

11. Build a small thread dam to prop the wing upright. Do *not* post the wing; just build the thread dam to stand it up.

12. Select a hackle feather that has fibers equal to about one-and-a-half hook gaps. Prepare the feather by stripping the butt end so the quill is exposed for a length of about two-thirds of a shank length.

13. Tie the hackle feather in with the outside of the feather up in front of the wing, and wrap back over the stem with the thread to the base of the wing.

14. Pull the hackle feather straight up and then slightly in front of the wing. The feather should tangle in the wing a bit and stay out of the way in the meantime.

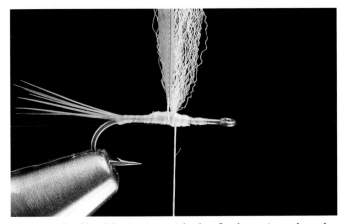

15. Detail of hackle tie-in, with the feather pinned to the wing.

16. Apply a thin strand of dubbing to the thread and begin wrapping it with the first turn of dubbing at the bend of the hook.

17. Work the dubbing forward to the 40 percent point on the hook. You should still have a length of dubbing on the thread during this process.

18. Pull the hackle feather back along the hook shank and bind it down with the dubbed thread as you continue forward up to the 75 percent point with the dubbing.

19. Continue forward with the dubbing (over the bare hackle stem) up to, and in front of, the wing. Stop the dubbing at the 75 to 80 percent point, leaving a bit of bare shank in front of it.

20. Place a drop of thin vinyl cement at the base of the wing.

21. Allow the cement to bleed down into the dubbing at the base of the wing as shown.

22. Spread the wing into a fan shape while the cement is still wet.

23. Quickly now, before the cement dries, palmer the hackle forward with two or three turns behind the wing right over the wet cement.

24. Continue wrapping the hackle feather forward in front of the wing for another two or three turns.

25. Tie the feather off at the front of the dubbing and clip the excess.

26. Apply another thin strand of dubbing to the thread and wrap it from the rear edge of the hook eye back to the front of the last turn of hackle.

27. Bring the dubbed thread forward again with a few turns, creating a smoothly tapered head.

28. Whip-finish and clip the thread.

29. Trim the wing to about one shank-length long.

30. Trim a notch out of the bottom of the hackle, forming a V-shape cutout. Test the fly on a hard surface to make sure it sits upright.

31. The finished fly.

PATTERN VARIATIONS

CHARLIE CRAVEN

VIS-A-DUN
(PMD)

Hook:	Size 16–24 Tiemco 101
Thread:	Light cahill 8/0 Uni-Thread
Tail:	Watery dun hackle fibers
Wing:	Light gray poly yarn
Abdomen:	PMD Superfine dubbing
Hackle:	Light dun rooster
Thorax:	PMD Superfine dubbing
Head:	PMD Superfine dubbing
Adhesive:	Wapsi vinyl cement

CHARLIE CRAVEN

VIS-A-DUN
(Trico)

Hook:	Size 18–24 Tiemco 101
Thread:	Black 8/0 Uni-Thread
Tail:	Watery dun hackle fibers
Wing:	Light gray poly yarn
Abdomen:	Black Superfine dubbing
Hackle:	Grizzly rooster
Thorax:	Black Superfine dubbing
Head:	Black Superfine dubbing
Adhesive:	Wapsi vinyl cement

CHARLIE CRAVEN

VIS-A-DUN
(Melon Dun)

Hook:	Size 18–24 Tiemco 101
Thread:	Rusty brown 8/0 Uni-Thread
Tail:	Watery dun hackle fibers
Wing:	Light gray poly yarn
Abdomen:	Cinnamon Superfine dubbing
Hackle:	Light dun rooster
Thorax:	Cinnamon Superfine dubbing
Head:	Cinnamon Superfine dubbing
Adhesive:	Wapsi vinyl cement

CHAPTER 15

Web Wing Caddis

There are approximately 1,400 species of caddis in the United States. They live in just about all of the water that we fish, and are an important food source for the trout. They can hatch from early spring through the late fall. They undergo a complete metamorphosis—egg, larva, pupa, and adult. After they emerge, adult caddis can live for up to a month, and, unlike mayflies, they can feed and drink. They are tough little organisms. They actually have a life.

When fishermen talk about caddis hatches they usually talk about the adult, but as I mentioned in the chapter on my caddis pupae, fish eat far more pupae than adults during a hatch because the pupae are much easier targets. They drift in the water while they ascend the water column to hatch, making them vulnerable to trout.

Many caddis adults leave the water shortly after shedding their pupal shucks. They usually don't float down the river for a while like mayflies. The only rivers I have seen adult caddis drift on the surface for a long time, and where the trout were feeding on them, are the Missouri and the Big Horn (back when it had impressive black caddis hatches and the fish loved to rise). I know there are other rivers where the caddis stay on the surface after hatching, because I have heard stories about them. Many caddis hatch at night, which makes for difficult dry-fly fishing. Most often we see caddis flying around or sitting in the bushes. Caddis hatches can be prolific, and all of the adults don't immediately leave the water surface. Gusts of wind can drive adult caddis to the surface of the water.

Trout see plenty of adult caddis, and they readily take adult caddis patterns. Adult caddis return to the river to lay eggs. They either skitter across the surface and drop their eggs, or they swim or dive under the surface and deposit their eggs on the bottom, or in some cases on our waders. Many of us have finished an evening fishing and found green clumps of caddis eggs on our waders.

The Web Wing Caddis came about because I needed a durable and realistic adult caddis pattern. Duck and turkey quill wings are realistic enough, but the fibers in the feather separate and the wing loses its shape after a

CHARLIE CRAVEN

WEB WING CADDIS
(Tan)

Hook:	Size 14–20 Tiemco 101
Thread:	Brown or tan 8/0 Uni-Thread
Hackle:	Grizzly rooster neck or saddle
Body:	Dark tan Superfine dubbing
Wing:	Mottled tan Web Wing

few fish—even if you apply vinyl cement to the wing. Over the years I tried different synthetics, but none of them worked for a variety of reasons. The material was either too fragile or didn't hold its shape.

I found the perfect material when Web Wing was introduced by D's Flies in Denver, Colorado. It comes in a good variety of colors, both plain and mottled, it is durable, and keeps its shape after numerous fish. It is effective on pressured fish in flat water as well as fish in broken water. Its one shortcoming is that in riffles it is sometimes difficult to see, especially if the light is not good, but I overcome that by fishing it behind a visible fly such as a Vis-A-Dun. Mayfly activity often accompanies caddis activity, so a mayfly-caddis combination that represents what has been hatching or is hatching can be effective.

This nice Roaring Fork rainbow ate one of the first prototypes of the Web Wing Caddis trailed behind a Vis-A-Dun.
ROSS PURNELL

If the trout aren't interested in mayflies and are totally focused on caddis, a better choice for the first fly is another caddis pattern. I use Mike Lawson's E-Z Caddis if I need a highly visible caddis imitation, but if the light is good I'll fish double Web Wing Caddis patterns or a Web Wing Caddis with a Graphic Caddis dropper. Even if caddis are not actually hatching while you are fishing, but you see them flying around or they are in the streamside vegetation, a Web Wing Caddis with a Graphic Caddis dropper can be effective for blind-casting. If there are numerous adults around, you can bet that the trout have eaten lots of pupae and adults and will readily accept good imitations of both.

When fishing the Web Wing Caddis, a dead drift is often best, but an occasional twitch can sometimes trigger a take, especially if there are egg-laying caddis around. I carry the pattern in sizes 14-20. I don't carry flies that are large enough to imitate the giant October caddis, but if you know you may encounter these, have a few larger patterns in your box. As with any dry fly, size is most important, and the color only needs to be close. I tie the pattern in tan, brown, and dark dun. One of these three colors covers most of the caddis I most often encounter.

When Web Wing was introduced by D's Flies out of Denver, Colorado, I found the perfect material for an adult caddis pattern. Web Wing comes in a good variety of colors, both plain and mottled, it is durable, and it keeps its shape after numerous fish. It is effective on pressured fish in flat water as well as fish in broken water. From left to right: dun, brown, and tan Web Wing Caddis.
CHARLIE CRAVEN

WEB WING CADDIS

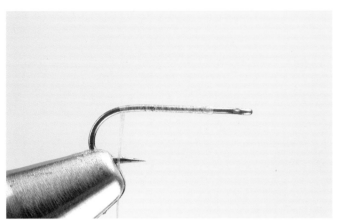

1. Insert the hook into the vise. Start the tying thread slightly behind the hook eye and wrap a smooth thread base back to the bend.

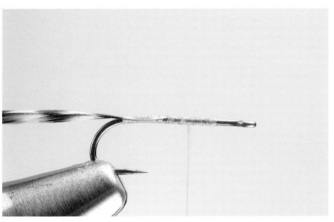

2. Size and prepare a hackle feather with barbs that are slightly longer than a gap width, and tie it in at the bend of the hook by the butt end with the outside of the feather facing up.

3. Apply dubbing to the thread and wrap the dubbing from the hook bend to about one eye length back from the hook eye, forming a level abdomen.

4. Palmer the hackle feather forward over the dubbed body and tie it off at the front edge of the body. Clip the excess hackle feather flush with the shank here.

5. Clip the hackle across the top of the fly as close as you can. I clip the top edges a bit, too, in order to allow the wing to sit down over the body. Make a thread base over the shank from the front edge of the body to the hook eye and back again.

6. Cut a strip of Web Wing from the sheet that is about twice as wide as the hook gap. Fold the sheet in half and run your thumbnail over it to crease the strip. Fold this strip over the hook with the front edge right behind the hook eye and pinch it in place.

7. Tie the Web Wing down with a pinch wrap at the front edge of the body. Wrap over the exposed stub end to form a smooth thread head.

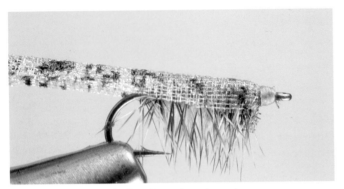

8. Whip-finish and clip the tying thread.

9. Trim the back of the wing at a 45-degree angle from the bottom to the top, forming the familiar tent-shaped caddis wing. Apply a bead of superglue along the top of the Web Wing to bond it to the dubbing.

10. Side view of the wing shape.

PATTERN VARIATIONS

CHARLIE CRAVEN

WEB WING CADDIS
(Brown)

Hook:	Size 14–20 Tiemco 101
Thread:	Brown 8/0 Uni-Thread
Hackle:	Brown rooster neck or saddle
Body:	Blue-Winged Olive Superfine dubbing
Wing:	Mottled brown Web Wing

CHARLIE CRAVEN

WEB WING CADDIS
(Dun)

Hook:	Size 14–20 Tiemco 101
Thread:	Iron gray 8/0 Uni-Thread
Hackle:	Grizzly rooster neck or saddle
Body:	Olive Superfine dubbing
Wing:	Mottled dark dun Web Wing

CHAPTER 16

B/C Hopper

In the spring, grasshopper eggs laid the previous fall hatch from the ground into little tiny wingless versions of the mature adults. The baby hoppers molt through the spring until they are fully grown with a set of wings and strong hindlegs by summer. I'm not sure how many different species live around trout habitat, but I don't think it's important. A hopper is a hopper, and they come in a variety of sizes and colors. Like beetles and ants, they are terrestrial but often land in the water where they are eaten by trout. The mature adult stage is the only stage that is important to fly fishers.

Hoppers live for months after they mature. They live into the fall until a hard freeze kills them. Under the right circumstances, they can be an important food source, and their patterns are fun to fish. Good hopper fishing is cyclical: some years are good, and others are terrible. The main reason for bad hopper years is if there is a hard freeze after they hatch, most of them will die.

As their name implies, grasshoppers' preferred habitat is grass. To have good hopper fishing, grass must border the river. A good way to gauge the hopper population around a river you are going to fish is the number of hoppers you spook as you are walking through the grass along or near the riverbank. When spooked, a hopper will either fly or jump; in either case they will show themselves. If you are spooking lots of hoppers, you may be in for a good day of hopper fishing, but good hopper fishing can be hard to come by. There may be numerous hoppers in the grass but they must end up in the water for the trout to be on the lookout for them. For a good number of hoppers to end up in the water, you usually need some really strong winds. It helps a great deal if there is something spooking the hoppers so that when they are airborne, the wind can blow them into the water. The hoppers can be spooked by cattle, tractors, or humans walking through the grass and inadvertently kicking up the hoppers.

Even with no wind, hoppers fly without being spooked and sometimes mistakenly land on the water. Also if there has been a lot of wind when there is a good hopper population, chances are the trout have seen and eaten some hoppers and will keep an eye out for them.

CHARLIE CRAVEN

B/C HOPPER
(Tan)

Hook:	Size 6–10 Tiemco 5262
Thread:	Tan 3/0 monocord
Body:	Tan 3mm foam
Binder Strip:	Tan 3mm foam
Adhesive:	Zap-A-Gap
Hopper Legs:	Tan round rubber leg
Underwing:	Mottled tan Web Wing
Flash:	Rootbeer Krystal Flash
Overwing:	Elk hair
Bullet Head:	Natural deer hair
Front Legs:	Tan round rubber legs
Indicator:	Pink McFlylon or Float Viz

Usually for a trout to eat hopper patterns they have to have seen and eaten some naturals. Hopper fishing begins when you start to see them and ends when you don't, which is usually around the first hard frost of autumn.

Before the B/C Hopper, I tied a hopper inspired by Mike Lawson's original Henry's Fork Hopper but modified by using Madam X style rubber legs, turkey quill for the flat wing, and an elk-hair overwing. I used elk hair

The B/C Hopper was a combined effort between Charlie Craven and me. I tie it in tan, yellow, and orange. The orange and yellow do double-duty as adult stonefly imitations. CHARLIE CRAVEN

for the body and bullet head and tied it on size 6–10 3XL hook. If my timing on a particular river was good, it was an effective pattern. I remember years ago on the Big Horn, when there was an all-out hopper bite, it hammered trout when fished along grassy banks.

But the pattern had some shortcomings. Even after applying several coats of vinyl cement to the turkey quill wing, it would still separate and the fibers would splay out in all directions after hooking a few fish. The elk hair required to tie the pattern needed to be very long, especially in the larger sizes, and quality long elk hair was difficult to come by. Also the body was not very durable. After a number of fish, the fibers could be cut and the fly would lose its buoyancy.

Despite its limitations, I continued to fish the pattern until Jackson Streit introduced me to the Hopper-Dropper approach. I realized then that I needed a new version that floated high and had a more durable body and wing. Closed-cell foam was the best choice for the body. The only foam pattern I tied was a beetle. I turned to the foam guru, Charlie Craven, for assistance. He was the master at foam hopper bodies, as is evidenced by his pattern the Charlie Boy Hopper. (The Charlie Boy Hopper is an excellent hopper but too small to support heavy droppers.) He came up with a body that was

durable, buoyant, and the wing laid in nicely over the body. About the same time a material called Web Wing became available. It was a great replacement for the turkey quill underwing; it held its shape while fishing, and was durable. The legs on the original pattern that I tied were Madame X style. Charlie tricked up the legs: he knotted the hind legs, and made them significantly larger than the small Madame X style forelegs. This change made the pattern's legs look just like a natural's, whose prominent feature is the rear legs. The B (Barr)/C (Craven) Hopper was finished.

Rarely have I encountered lots of fish feeding exclusively on grasshoppers, so I almost always have droppers under the hopper. In addition to being an important component to the Hopper-Copper-Dropper approach because of its bouyancy and high visibility, the B/C Hopper is an excellent hopper pattern on its own. The first fly I tie on below the B/C Hopper is always a Copper John with the second fly representing the prevailing insect activity. I usually fish the combination of flies dead drift, with a few twitches during the drift. If one of my droppers is a caddis pupa or mayfly emerger, I will hold the hopper stationary in the current, and let the nymphs swing up and rise to the surface at the end of the drift. I do the same thing when nymph-fishing.

Grassy banks are the classic place to throw hoppers. I have spent many enjoyable days drifting along in a boat casting the large flies toward the bank anticipating a big trout head coming up for the fly. Most people fish hoppers this way. But what I have come to realize is that fishing hoppers midstream can be just as, if not more, effective. Many hoppers are blown by the wind out into the main current flow, or mistakenly land out there. If there are hoppers around, trout away from the banks will have seen hoppers and will keep an eye out for them because they are a substantial and nutritious meal. I have caught many trout on hoppers by fishing out in the main current. In pressured fisheries, trout get conditioned to seeing hopper imitations thrown along the banks, but try throwing your hopper pattern out in the middle of the river, and the trout may let their guard down and take your hopper pattern. Not a lot of guys fish hoppers out in the river away from the banks.

I have had better success with smaller hoppers because the majority of the hoppers that live along stream banks are not very big. There are many sizes of hoppers around flowing waters, but the majority are size 8 or smaller. You will usually get more takes on a size 10 than a size 8, and more takes on a size 8 than a size 6. I have caught many trout on a size 6 when my Copper and Dropper require maximum buoyancy but many of the hoppers that live around rivers tend to be more in the size 10 range. If I am dropping a large Copper John, I will use a size 6 to support the heavy fly.

People have written about casting grasshopper imitations so that they hit the water hard. I have thrown many live hoppers into rivers and ponds and if they are mature hoppers they have wings and will fly. Sometimes they make it to the water and sometimes they just keep flying and get back to land. If they hit the water they land rather softly for a heavy insect. They don't just bomb in like a rock. Hoppers obviously don't hit the water like a delicate insect, but a normal cast is all that is needed. There is no need to pound them onto the surface—the size and weight of the fly gives all the impact on the water's surface that is necessary.

The B/C Hopper is durable and will keep its shape after many hours of fishing. After a number of fish, a few strands of elk hair on the head may get chewed through and stick out, but this does not affect how the fly floats or fishes. Also if you catch a bunch of fish on the fly, you can get tooth marks on the foam. The fly still fishes the same, and I kind of like the ones that have a bunch of tooth marks on them.

The closed-cell foam used in the B/C Hopper— and closed-cell foam in general—will not float forever because it absorbs water over time. After a while the

CHARLIE MEYERS

CHARLIE MEYERS

The B/C Hopper's main role is to support the Copper and Dropper in my three-fly system but it catches its share of fish, including panfish, bass, and trout. JOHN BARR

B/C Hopper can become waterlogged and lose the buoyancy to support heavy Copper Johns and Droppers. To prevent this, I usually tie on a fresh hopper about every three hours and put the old hopper aside. By the next day the foam will dry out and the fly will be as good as new.

To help keep the fly buoyant for the longest amount of time, I dress the foam and the other parts of the fly with a dry-fly dressing. Squirt the dressing on your fingers and rub it into the elk wing and the indictor material as well as completely covering the foam body. To rejuvenate the fly while I am fishing, and to help remove fish slime, I use Shimizake dry shake, which I think is an essential component of any fishing bag if you fish dry flies. Once you catch a fish, you'll find that the hopper, as well as other dry flies, doesn't float as well as it did before. Part of that is because the fly might have become waterlogged while you were playing the fish, you may have gotten weeds and algae on the fly, the slime from the fish may have matted the fly, or a combination of all three. To bring your fly back to new, simply place it (with the leader attached) in the bottle of Shimizake (or other comparable brand of desiccant) and shake briskly. The fly will look like new and float nice and high for you.

B/C HOPPER

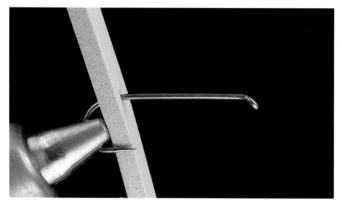

1. Begin by cutting a strip of foam about 4 inches long and as wide as the gap of the hook. Stretch the foam to make it a little more pliable and slightly thinner. Also at this time, cut a thin strip (about 3mm) of foam to use as a gluing surface on the hook shank. Pierce the strip of body foam about 1 inch from the end with the hook point and thread the hook through the foam, then mount the hook in the vise.

2. Attach the thread to the hook and form a thread base from about three eye lengths back from the hook eye to the bend of the hook.

3. Return the thread to the three eye lengths back point and tie in the binder strip (gluing surface) along the top of the hook back to the bend. Be sure to bind this down tightly as this is what the body will be glued to.

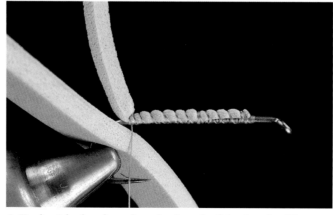

4. End with the thread at the bend of the hook. (Yes, you have had to work around the impaled strip of foam this whole time.)

5. Wrap the thread tightly back and forth over the foam strip to compress it down and give it some texture. This will be used as a gluing surface, so some "bite" is needed to adhere to.

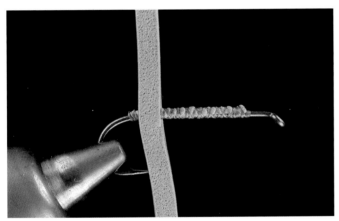

6. Slide the impaled strip of foam one foam width (3mm) past the base of the binder strip at the bend of the hook and pull the front of the strip under the hook toward the hook eye.

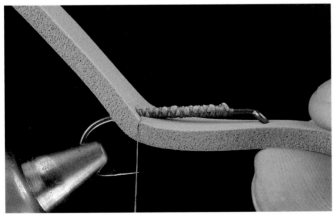

7. The thread should be hanging right here at the bend of the hook, just in front of the body strip.

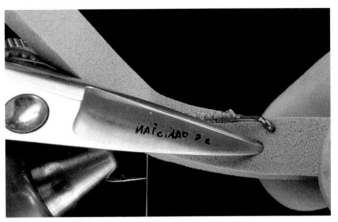

8. Make a hole in the foam with your scissor tips at the point where the foam intersects with the hook eye.

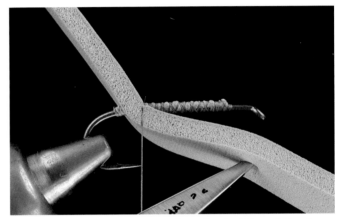

9. It helps to make the hole from both sides of the foam to ensure that it goes all the way through and doesn't close up.

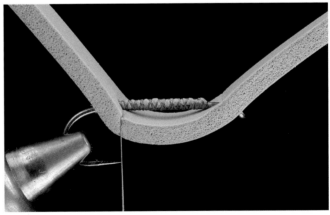

10. Push the hook eye through the new hole. You should now have the thread at the bend and the foam threaded onto the hook in two places (just behind the eye and the bend).

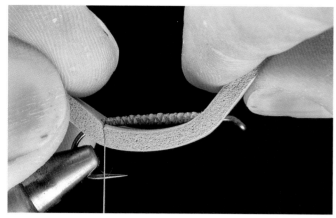

11. Grasp the foam strip at the front and back and slide the whole strip back to the bend of the hook so there is about 3mm of space at the front of the hook between the eye and the foam.

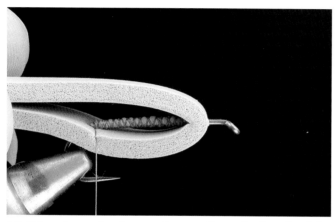

12. Note how the 3mm of space from the bend of the hook has now been magically moved to the front.

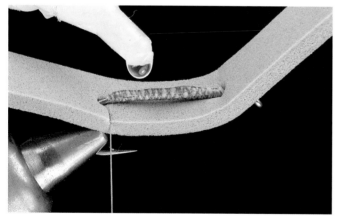

13. Now apply a thin coat of Zap-A-Gap to the entire upper surface of the foam.

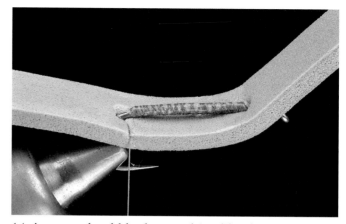

14. Amount should look something like this.

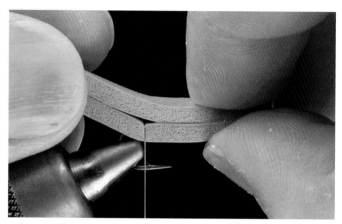

15. Next, before the glue dries, fold the foam that is protruding forward from the hook eye back over the top of the hook and press both halves together. Hold the two halves together until the glue grabs.

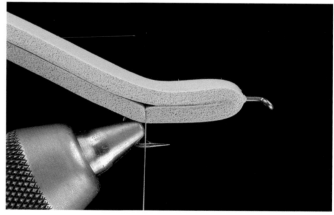

16. Once the glue has dried a bit, the two halves of the foam should look like this. Note the thread sticking out of the near side of the body at the bend of the hook.

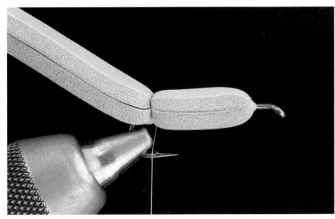

17. Now, at the bend, make three to five turns of thread on top of each other tightly to form the start of the first segment.

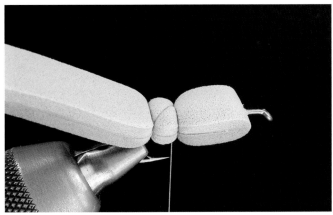

18. Now, to work the thread forward, cross the thread diagonally across the top of the body one time, then make two to three more turns to create the next segment. These turns should be almost vertical.

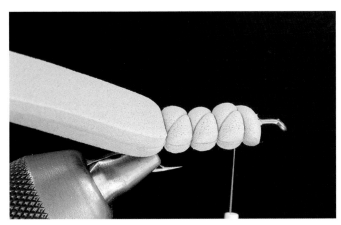

19. Continue forward making three segments, all evenly spaced and equal in length, and a fourth segment at the front end that is a little shorter than the other three.

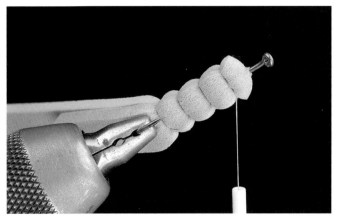

20. View of the underside. The crossing travel wraps should only show on the top of the body, while the bottom side will only show the even segments.

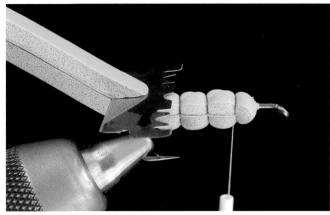

21. Now pull the extended body portion of the foam up and with half of a double-edge razor blade make a cut along the extended body portion of the foam straight back to form a diagonal body shape. Make one clean cut.

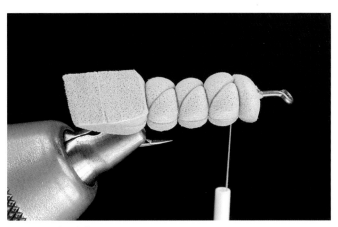

22. Detail of first cut.

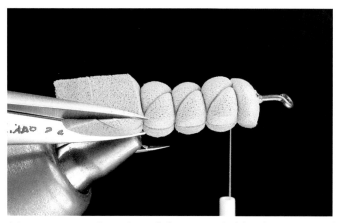

23. Now trim the sides of the extended body section of the foam on each side so that the extended portion is the same width as the foam body that is tied onto the hook.

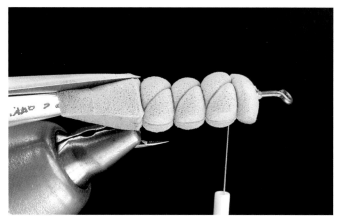

24. Trim the other side.

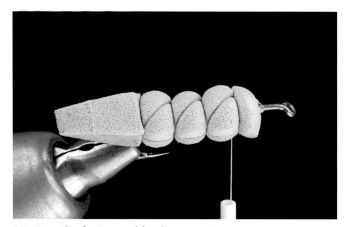

25. Detail of trimmed body extension.

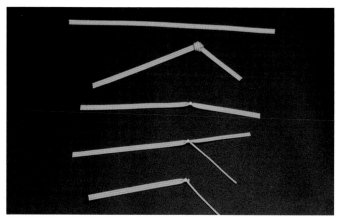

26. Take three strands of tan rubber legs about three inches long and *without* separating them, tie them in an overhand knot to form the kicker legs. Do this to another piece for the other leg. Trim off two of the three strands on one side of the knot for the lower leg section.

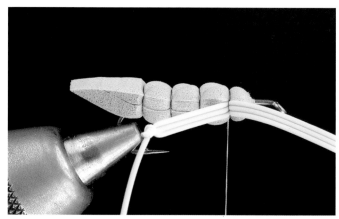

27. With the thread at the front of the first body segment, tie in one leg with two or three turns of thread.

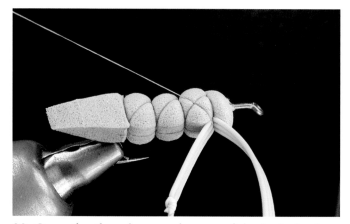

28. Cross the thread across the top of the body back to the next segment back.

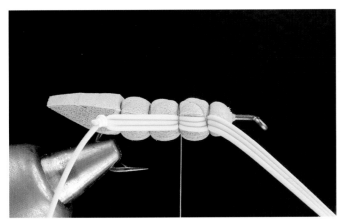

29. Bind the leg in again at that section. The "knee" should be even with the bend of the hook.

30. Now tie in the other leg on the opposite side starting from the second segment, binding the leg in place.

31. Cross the top of the body to the first segment and tie the leg down again at this point.

32. Detail of far side leg tie-in.

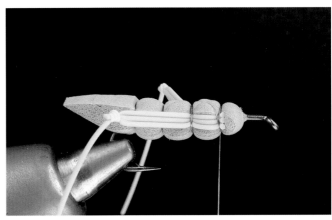

33. Trim the butt ends (three-strand end) off flush with the body on both sides.

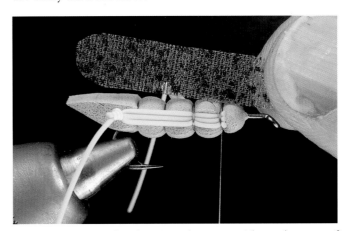

34. Cut a piece of Web Wing about as wide as the gap of the hook and trim the end into a rounded shape. This will form the underwing.

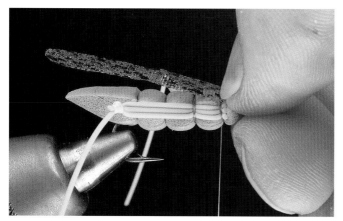

35. Tie in the Web Wing at the front of the first segment so the rounded end extends past the end of the body about a quarter of the body length.

37. Take three or four long strands of Krystal Flash and double them over the thread to make eight strands. Tie these in on top of the base of the under wing. These should extend just past the bend as well.

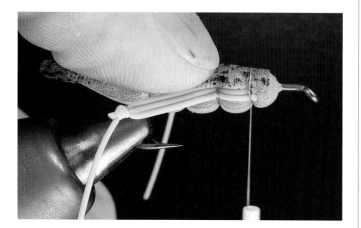

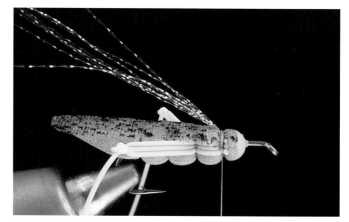

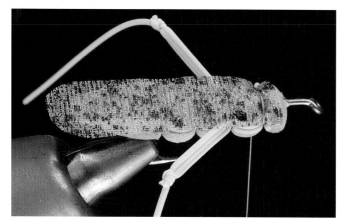

36. Detail of Web Wing tie-in.

38. Clean and stack a clump of elk hair and measure it against the shank so it extends back to the bend of the hook.

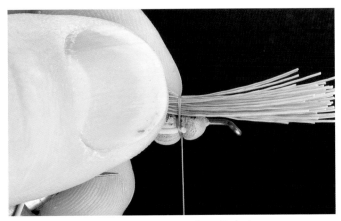

39. Make three light turns over the elk hair.

40. Then pull straight down on the thread to flare the butts.

41. Trim the butt ends of the elk hair wing, leaving a short stub like you would on an Elk Hair Caddis. This butt end will act as an anchor and prevent the hair from slipping out later.

42. Make a thread base all the way up to the hook eye, then back again to the front of the foam body and return it once more to just behind the hook eye.

Cut and clean a large clump of deer body hair. Stack the hair and measure the clump against the shank so it is as long as the hook shank. The tips should be facing toward the front of the fly.

43. Cut the clump of deer hair so it is equal to one shank length long and place the butt ends of the clump above the hook, right behind the hook eye. The butts should extend about ¼ inch past the thread.

44. Make three turns of thread around this clump of deer hair. The first turn should have just enough tension to crease the hair and the subsequent two turns should lie right on top of the first turn.

45. Release the clump of hair from your fingertips and hold onto the hook shank with your material hand.

48. and to the notch in the base of the elk hair wing.

46. Pull slightly back and down with the thread, spinning the hair completely around the hook shank. You can manually distribute the hair (help it along) if it is less than cooperative in the spinning process.

49. Let the thread hang on the bobbin.

47. Work the tying thread back through the butt ends of the hair . . .

50. Spread the deer hair around the shank so it radiates out from the hook eye as shown. You want a complete 360-degree collar of deer hair at the front of the hook.

51. Push the end of a Bic pen tube back over the hair, forcing the hair back to the thread. You may need to rock the pen back and forth a bit to compress the hair. Push the end of the pen all the way back to the thread.

52. With the pen still in place against the thread, make a turn of thread around the hair where it exits the pen tube. Make a couple tight wraps here, flaring the collar.

53. Pull the pen tube off the front of the fly, exposing the perfect bullet head. Yours came out just like this, didn't it?

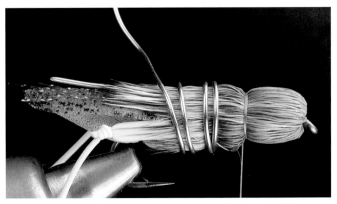

54. Grasp all the deer hair in the collar, as well as the wing and back legs, and pinch them down against the body of the fly. Wrap a few turns of heavy lead wire around the hook to hold these parts out of the way while you tie the rest of the fly.

55. Cut a 2-inch-long piece of round rubber leg and tie it in at the center of its length at the base of the bullet head with two turns of thread. From this point on, there are minimal thread turns required to tie each piece in, as they become cumulative. Everything is tied in in the same place, so the wraps pile up a bit. Be sparing with the thread turns!

56. Tie in another piece of rubber leg along the far side of the head in the same manner as the first. Turn the fly in the vise so you can make sure that the legs are on the sides of the head and centered.

57. Brush out a heavy clump of pink McFlylon and tie it in on top of the bullet head at the base of the collar for the indicator.

58. Clip the front end of the McFlylon into a short stub. Don't bother to try to cover the butts; just leave them exposed at the front. They will anchor the indicator and keep it from pulling out later.

59. Clip the yarn.

60. Whip-finish the thread on top of the tie-down area at the base of the collar. Clip the thread.

61. Remove the lead.

62. Trim the back legs so they are about two-thirds of a shank length long.

63. Pull the deer hair on the bottom of the collar down and trim it flush against the body, exposing the foam underbody.

64. Run a bead of head cement all the way around the thread collar.

65. Use permanent markers to mottle the legs a bit. Mottling simulates movement and makes the fly buggier, and who can say it doesn't look better with the markings?

66. Finished fly, top view.

67. Bottom view.

68. Front view.

69. Side view.

PATTERN VARIATIONS

B/C HOPPER
(Yellow)

Hook:	Size 6–10 Tiemco 5262
Thread:	Yellow 3/0 monocord
Body:	Yellow 3mm foam
Binder Strip:	Yellow 3mm foam
Adhesive:	Zap-A-Gap
Hopper Legs:	Yellow round rubber leg
Underwing:	Mottled hopper yellow Web Wing
Flash:	Yellow Krystal Flash
Overwing:	Elk hair
Bullet Head:	Yellow deer hair
Front Legs:	Yellow round rubber legs
Indicator:	Hot orange McFlylon or Float Viz

B/C HOPPER
(Orange)

Hook:	Size 6–10 Tiemco 5262
Thread:	Black 3/0 monocord
Body:	Orange 3mm foam
Binder Strip:	Orange 3mm foam
Adhesive:	Zap-A-Gap
Hopper Legs:	Black round rubber leg
Underwing:	Mottled gray Web Wing
Flash:	Orange Krystal Flash
Overwing:	Elk hair
Bullet Head:	Black deer hair
Front Legs:	Black round rubber legs
Indicator:	Hot orange McFlylon or Float Viz

CHAPTER 17

Drowned Spinner

As I wrote in the Vis-A-Dun chapter, after mayflies hatch into duns, they eventually transform into spinners, the stage in which they reproduce. Once the spinners mate, the females fly over the water's surface where they deposit eggs that eventually sink to the bottom. Some species, most notably *Baetis,* dive or swim under the surface and deposit their eggs on the bottom. After mating and laying their eggs, the spinners die. Many end up on the surface of the water, a phenomenon anglers call a spinner fall, and can provide excellent fishing. Most spinner falls occur in the morning or evening.

The place that I have spent the most time fishing Trico spinner falls and learning about the hatch was on the South Platte between Spinney and Elevenmile Reservoirs. I named this stretch the Dream Stream because it was an incredible fishery with lots of big fish and it had varied and consistent hatches, providing dependable dry-fly fishing from late spring through the fall. Spring through summer, you could expect *Baetis,* PMD, and caddis hatches, and toward the end of June, the Tricos started hatching. The Trico spinner falls created predictable and excellent fishing for rising trout almost every morning through September and sometimes into October.

For years when I fished a mayfly spinner fall, I fished a single floating spinner representing the natural that was on the water. I have fished Trico spinner falls on the Colorado, Big Horn, Henry's Fork, Missouri, and other rivers. I would manage to catch some fish during a Trico spinner fall, but I found that I had to make many casts and strike blindly to catch a few fish. Fishing a spinner pattern that lies flush in the surface film was often frustrating. If the lighting was not perfect, it was difficult to see the fly, and I often had to strike if a fish rose near where I gauged my fly to be and hope I got lucky. Usually I guessed wrong and came up empty-handed. It was also frustrating because I was never exactly sure whether the fly was floating totally drag-free, which is absolutely essential when fishing spinners. Spinners are dead and motionless. Finally, spinner falls, especially Trico spinner falls, are often heavy and the many naturals blanketing

DROWNED SPINNER
(Rusty)

Hook:	Size 14–22 Tiemco 2488H
Thread:	Rusty brown 6/0 Danville
Tail:	Pale watery dun hackle fibers
Abdomen:	Tying thread
Wings:	White Antron yarn
Thorax:	Copper Quick Descent dubbing

the water significantly decreases the odds that a trout will take the single imitation.

In the late 1990s, my approach to fishing spinner falls changed dramatically. On a day in early September while fishing the Dream Stream, I had a fair day fishing the Trico spinner fall. After the spinner fall had ended and I could find no more rising trout, I decided to head back to my truck. I was walking along the bank, returning to my vehicle, when I spotted a nice brown holding in the current. I half-heartedly flipped my spinner to him, but it sank. I said to myself, "swell." To my surprise, the brown came up and took the submerged spinner. At that moment, I realized that fish must be accustomed to seeing drowned spinners.

Landon Mayer casting to trout feeding on Tricos on the Yampa River. JOHN BARR

Drowned, or sunken, spinners are often overlooked by anglers, but trout don't miss them. Many spinners swim underwater to lay their eggs, and others are washed under the water's surface by turbulent currents. Trout love to stack up downstream of a riffle that shelves off and gorge on drowned spinners. From left to right: rusty, pale olive, and Trico Drowned Spinners.
CHARLIE CRAVEN

The spinner is the stage that mates and lays eggs. Spinners have clear wings. Mating swarms of spinners dancing in the air are popular sights on trout streams across the country. After mating, the females of most species fly along the water's surface and deposit their eggs. Some, like *Baetis* (Blue-Winged Olives) dive or crawl under the surface and deposit their eggs on the bottom, and they eventually die and land on the water's surface. The female *Baetis* and other mayflies that lay their eggs on the bottom often die underwater, but a few can struggle back to the surface before they die. Spinners are easy meals because they are dead and can't move or fly off and they can bring on some excellent fishing.

During a spinner fall, one of the most impressive sights is all of the spent winged insects drifting on the surface of the water. But in many rivers there is turbulence and currents that sink some of the spinners. Some rivers are flat and may not have many drowned spinners, but the trout will still usually take a sunken spinner pattern without hesitation. There are also far fewer drowned naturals to compete with your pattern.

Instead of a pattern that was tied with a standard dry-fly hook using materials that floated, I needed a pattern that would sink. I used a 2XS shank and a 3X wide gapped curved hook. The hook resulted in a small fly with much better hooking capabilities than the standard dry-fly hook, which has a standard-sized gap.

I used pale watery dun hackle fibers for the tail, a thread abdomen coated with head cement, and after a few years a thorax of Quick Descent dubbing when it became available. The first trout I caught on a drowned spinner did not have Quick Descent dubbing—it was just a standard spinner that happened to sink. Before Quick Descent dubbing came along I just tied the thorax with thread, which sank, but not as well as Quick Descent made from metal.

The Quick Descent is made from aluminum shavings. The wing is tied with white Antron, which sinks and becomes almost transparent when wet, yet glows when hit by the sunlight. That glow seems to attract the trout. I tied three versions of the drowned spinner: black for Tricos, and rust and olive for the other species such as PMDs and *Baetis*.

My drowned spinner not only imitates spinners that are submerged under the water's currents, but also imitates the few species of mayflies that actually dive underwater to lay their eggs, such as *Baetis*. For years *Baetis* spinners were a total enigma to me. I wondered why with such prolific hatches in the spring and fall—sometimes bank to bank, especially on cloudy days—I never saw a commensurately heavy spinner fall. In 2004 the mystery

This brown took a Drowned Trico Spinner fished under a Trico Vis-A-Dun—one of my favorite combinations for fishing Trico spinnerfalls. LANDON MAYER

was unraveled. After talking with Mike Lawson and Kelly Galloup and seeing some photos in *Fly Fisherman,* I learned that *Baetis* spinners dive or crawl under the surface and lay their eggs on the bottom. If there has been *Baetis* activity, a small rusty-bodied pattern with a sparse Antron wing tied in over the body can be an effective nymph. This pattern represents the drowned *Baetis* spinner. Mike and Kelly like a little soft-hackle pattern.

During a spinner fall with rising fish, I fish a drowned spinner most of the time, tied off the bend of a Vis-A-Dun matching the dun of the mayfly that produced the spinner on the water. The Vis-A-Dun acts as a strike indicator and a drag detector. I hang the drowned spinner off the bend of the dry fly with 6 to 8 inches of tippet. I fish 6X fluorocarbon to both the dry fly and drowned spinner. For Trico spinner falls I fish a

If fish are rising during a spinner fall, I usually fish a Drowned Spinner instead of a floating one. I tie it off the back of a Vis-A-Dun on 6 to 8 inches of 6X tippet.

black-bodied Vis-A-Dun with a drowned Trico Spinner tied off the bend. Fish will often take the Vis-A-Dun when fishing a spinner fall. I think at the right angle the dun looks like a spinner. The most prominent feature of a Trico spinner is the black body. With the wings and tails being almost invisible, the black body of the dun must be what generates the takes.

You may not always be lucky enough to be on the water during a spinner fall, but if there has been mayfly dun activity, there's a good chance trout have seen spinners. Even if there are no spinners on the water at the time you are fishing, trout certainly recognize them, and an appropriate drowned spinner is an excellent choice as a nymph.

"Another great pattern John introduced me to is his Drowned Trico Spinner. Up on the Missouri River a few years ago, John was just slaying the big fish, while I was having trouble getting them to take a standard hen hackle Trico spinner. He wouldn't tell me his secret all afternoon—just let me suffer. Then I could see that he was fishing an odd rig with one high-riding fly and another that looked like it was sinking. I should have known. The sinking fly was the Drowned Trico Spinner, and John was using a big oversized Trico dun for the indicator! It was a deadly rig for sure and I accused him of fishing wet flies when we were supposed to be fishing dry flies and spinners. The fact that he was catching three fish to my one didn't seem to bother him. After that I started using the Drowned Trico Spinner myself, especially when things got tough and the fish ignored a standard spinner."

—GEORGE ANDERSON, Yellowstone Angler,
Livingston, Montana

DROWNED SPINNER

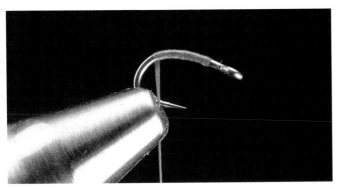

1. Insert the hook into the vise. Start the tying thread behind the eye and wrap a smooth thread base slightly down the bend of the hook.

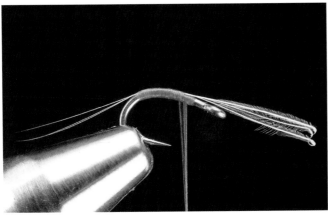

2. Tie in three pale dun hackle fibers for the tail that are about 1 ½ shanks long.

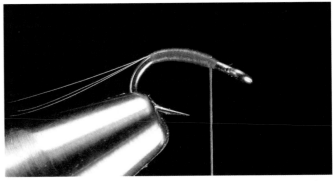

3. Clip the butt ends of the tails and build a smooth, thin thread base over them for the abdomen.

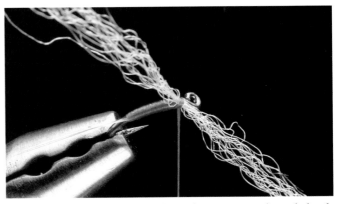

4. Move the thread forward to about an eye length back from the hook eye. Tie in a length of Antron yarn, with two diagonal wraps from the back side of the base of the near wing to the front side of the base of the far wing.

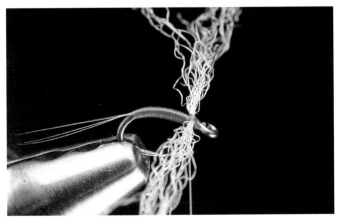

5. Pull the Antron so it is perpendicular to the shank and make another two diagonal wraps. This time they should go from the front of the near wing to the back of the far wing base. These wraps will lock the wings into their horizontal position, perpendicular to the hook.

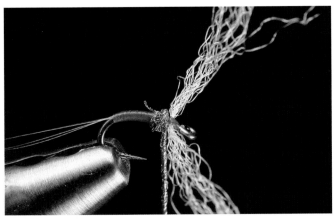

6. Dub the thread with a small amount of Quick Descent dubbing and begin wrapping it behind the wings as shown. Wrap up the back edge of the wings.

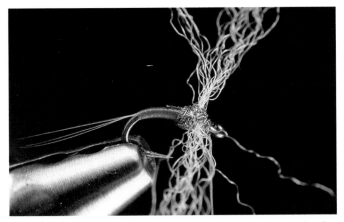

7. Make a figure-eight through the wings with the dubbed thread, and continue forward to just behind the hook eye, forming a bulbous thorax. Whip-finish and clip the thread.

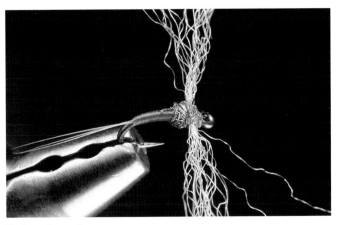

8. Another view.

9. Pull the Antron wings back toward the bend of the hook and trim them even with the end of the body.

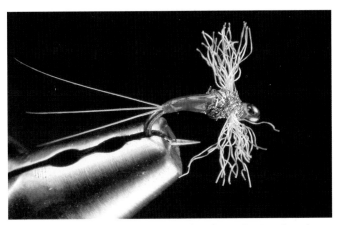

10. Push your thumbnail up under the tails to splay them out a bit. Coat the abdomen with a couple coats of Sally Hansen's Hard As Nails.

PATTERN VARIATIONS

CHARLIE CRAVEN

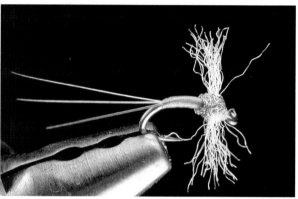

CHARLIE CRAVEN

DROWNED SPINNER
(Trico)

Hook:	Size 14–22 Tiemco 2488H
Thread:	Black 6/0 Danville
Tail:	Pale watery dun hackle fibers
Abdomen:	Tying thread
Wings:	White Antron yarn
Thorax:	Black Quick Descent dubbing

DROWNED SPINNER
(Pale Olive)

Hook:	Size 14–22 Tiemco 2488H
Thread:	Light cahill 8/0 Uni-Thread
Tail:	Pale watery dun hackle fibers
Abdomen:	Tying thread
Wings:	White Antron yarn
Thorax:	Gold Quick Descent dubbing

CHAPTER 18

Slumpbuster

Years ago, a fisheries biologist told me that once brown trout reach 16 or 17 inches long, their primary forage is baitfish. Baitfish are any fish that they can swallow, whether it is a sculpin or a juvenile brown trout. That's not to say baitfish is all they eat; they will eat nymphs and occasionally adult aquatic insects on the surface—most notably large insects such as green drakes and salmonflies—but their primary focus is baitfish. Once other species of trout become large, they will also focus on baitfish. Large fish need more nutrition than small fish and want to get the most food for energy expended.

Sometimes fish of all species will try to eat a fish larger than they can swallow, and choke to death on a fish that gets stuck in their throat. I have seen a dead pike with a big bass tail sticking out of its mouth; I have seen a dead 4-pound bass with a 2-pound bass half sticking out of its mouth. I caught a nice brown with a 6-inch chub lodged in its throat. Why he ate my nymph is a mystery. At any rate, I am sure his life was spared when I extracted the chub and released him. The bottom line is: big fish like a substantial meal. The reason some fly fishermen like to spend a lot of time streamer fishing is that, on the average, they are going to catch larger fish than nymph or dry-fly fishermen.

I created the Slumpbuster to look like a baitfish. Some streamer patterns have lots of glitz, flash, rubber legs, and materials that don't look natural, but do produce reaction strikes. A reaction strike is when a fly comes ripping past a fish and they can't help but take a snap at it for whatever reason, but surely not because it looks like anything they have been eating. When wet, the Slumpbuster has the perfect baitfish profile. It has subtle flash and looks alive in the water.

In 2000, Joe Schmuecker from Wapsi sent me some Zonker-cut pine squirrel skins dyed in a variety of colors as well as natural. I always get excited when I see a new material that is different from anything out there. Zonker strips have been around forever, but they have always come from rabbit, which has limitations due to its long hair. I started to envision patterns using the

CHARLIE CRAVEN

SLUMPBUSTER
(Olive)

Hook:	Size 4–12 Tiemco 5263
Thread:	Olive 70-denier Ultra Thread
Cone:	Gold tungsten, size 4–6 (large), size 8–10 (medium)
Rib:	Chartreuse Ultra Wire (Brassie)
Body:	Peacock Sparkle Braid
Wing/Tail:	Olive pine squirrel
Collar:	Olive pine squirrel

short-haired, nicely mottled pine squirrel strips. I tied a variety of prototypes, and finally ended up with one I really liked.

Lots of cool-looking patterns don't necessarily fish well, so I had to test mine onstream to see if the trout liked it. After one season, I knew it was a winner. It just flat-out caught fish. When wet, it has the perfect baitfish profile. It has subtle flash and looks alive in the water. Tricked-up streamers can often get follows or flashes, but fish don't eat them. When a pattern has lots of flash, rubber legs, and gaudy colors, trout, especially pressured fish, may show interest but can sense that something is

Most people pound the banks with streamers, but I often find it more productive to fish midriver. ROSS PURNELL

not quite right. Trout routinely try to actually eat the Slumpbuster.

One feature of the fly that adds to its durability and makes it a snap to tie is its uni-body construction. The tail, wing, and collar are all made from the same pine squirrel Zonker strip. The fly's durability comes from the fact that it is constructed with one primary material, that it is ribbed with Ultra Wire, and that I place a cyano-acrylate glue in the cone and jam it back into the collar. (Zap Gel is the best because it is viscous and will not run out of the cone and get on your desk and the collar of the fly.)

I fish the pattern year-round, but the best times are spring through fall. I fish at any time of the day whether it is sunny or cloudy, but the best time to fish for browns is early or late in the day.

I like to fish two Slumpbusters at the same time. I use 0X fluorocarbon tippet for both flies, with the second fly tied off the bend of the first fly on about 18 inches of tippet. The setup that I have the most confidence in is a size 4 natural color trailed by an olive, black, or rust in size 6. Sometimes I fish a size 6 trailed

Big trout eat baitfish. This North Platte brown was so gluttonous it continued to feed even though it had not yet swallowed a 6-inch chub. JOHN BARR

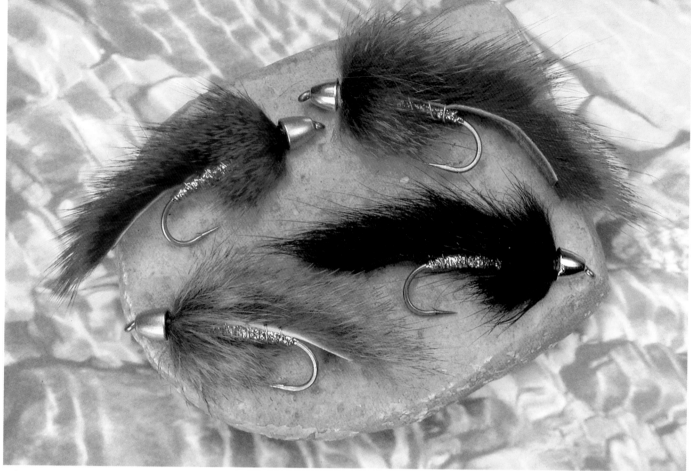

The Slumpbuster is tied with only a few materials and it is subtle. Tricked-up streamers can often get follows or flashes, but fish don't eat them. When a pattern has lots of flash, rubber legs, and gaudy colors, trout—especially pressured ones—show interest but can sense that something is not quite right. Trout routinely try to actually to eat the Slumpbuster. CHARLIE CRAVEN

by a size 8 or 10 if the trout want a smaller pattern. Let the trout tell you what size they want.

Anglers often fish streamers by casting toward the banks from a drift boat with sinking-tip lines. This approach can be effective, but in pressured waters the trout get conditioned to seeing flies cast to the bank and ripped back into the current and may just flash the streamer or not react at all. Good fish are caught doing this on pressured waters, but not with regularity. I have fished streamers from drift boats with the bank-pounding approach, and on pressured rivers have foul-hooked many small browns (which can be quite aggressive) on the second fly. The little browns were reacting to the flies, but not eating them. I have had unbelievable fishing while pounding the bank, but only in rivers with little pressure. Another traditional approach, often used by wade-fishermen is, using a sink tip, casting across and slightly downstream and swinging the streamer through a run. This approach has been successful for years and can be very rewarding. It does limit the way you can fish your streamer—you are limited to casting, swinging, and stripping, then picking up and doing the same thing again.

Nowadays, if I am streamer fishing pressured rivers from a drift boat, I most often cast my flies into the main

The Slumpbuster is an uncomplicated pattern to tie. One fly lasts for many fish primarily because the tail, wing, and collar are all made from the same pine squirrel Zonker strip.
JOHN BARR

My favorite Slumpbuster combination is a size 4 natural trailed by a size 6 olive, black, or rust.

This large brown ate a black Slumpbuster fished dead-drift.
LANDON MAYER

current. I usually fish streamers with a floating line and a 9-foot 0X leader. I cut off the 0X regular monofilament tippet and replace it with fluorocarbon. If all I did was fish streamers in rivers my entire leader would be fluoro-carbon; however, I use the same outfit fishing top water bass, for which I do not want to use a full sinking leader. It has been written that attaching a fluorocarbon leader to regular mono creates a weak connection. I have never found that to be the case. I have caught hundreds of large trout on 6X fluorocarbon tied to 5X monofilament. When dealing with 0X the knot strength is a non-factor.

The long leader allows the flies to sink rapidly. The Slumpbuster is heavy and two of them gives you plenty of weight to get the flies down in a hurry. You don't need a sink tip to get the flies down. The floating line gives you a lot more presentation options. I will throw to banks and swing it on a tight line occasionally, but my favorite and most productive way to fish the Slumpbuster—whether wade or drift boat fishing—is to cast slightly upstream, throw an upstream mend in the line, and let the flies sink. Trout love flies that are dropping. While I am fishing out a cast I keep throwing little mends and just let the flies drift along with an occasional twitch or slight strip. At the end of the drift, I let the flies swing until the line comes tight to the flies. I will give a couple of hard strips and cast again. A fish may be following the drifted and twitched flies and a couple of fast strips can sometimes produce some vicious takes. Many of my largest trout have come while the flies are dead-drifting.

To slow down the speed of the fly and sink it deeper, mend your line upstream.

The conventional way to fish streamers while wading is to cast across and downstream and swing your fly on a tight line, stripping in line to impart action to the fly. When fishing streamers from a drift boat, most anglers bomb the banks. I have a few different approaches that seem to work better on pressured trout. When wade fishing, I often cast upstream or across stream and throw a few mends into my fly line to sink my streamers deep. I'll then strip and twitch and dead-drift the fly until it swings below me. After it is swinging on a tight line, I strip in line to impart action to the fly. Sometimes, I high-stick the streamer like a nymph and then strip it as it swings downstream of me. When I fish from a boat, I also use this technique, and instead of casting toward the bank, I often focus on midstream pockets and shelves.

To detect the strikes while dead-drifting you can't have a lot of slack between your rod tip and the flies, or you will miss the take. This may require lifting the rod tip or subtle hand twists of the line. So it is not a true dead-drift like you get while indicator fishing with nymphs. I like to let the flies dive behind boulders and rocks and into depressions or off shelves. If I am fishing the bank and the water is shallow, I strip really fast so the flies don't get hung up on the bottom; then, when my flies come to a deeper water, I let the flies dive down the face of the drop-off. Trout love diving streamers. It is a motion they don't often see. The double Slumpbuster setup is not meant to be fished in really shallow water.

Rust is a good color, although there are not many rust-colored baitfish. I think trout may be taking the rust as a dead or molting crawdad. Keep in mind, sometimes we think trout are as intelligent as we are, and maybe they don't see the color rust very often, and they just want to give it a try. I do not have a definitive answer to why trout like the color rust; they just do. It is probably my favorite color streamer whether stripped or dead-drifted.

"The Slumpbuster is my all-time favorite fly. We always fish two streamers when hunting the big yellowfins (browns) and flesh-eating bows. A variety of streamers are used as the point fly, but they are always trailed by the Slump. We have caught more fish streamer fishing with the Slumpbuster than any other pattern."

—JASON HAMRICK, Cowboy Drifters,
Casper, Wyoming

SLUMPBUSTER

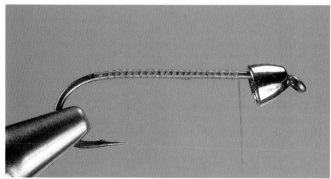

1. Place the cone on the hook and insert the hook into the vise. Start the thread about two eye lengths back. Wrap a thread base to the bend of the hook and return the thread to the starting point.

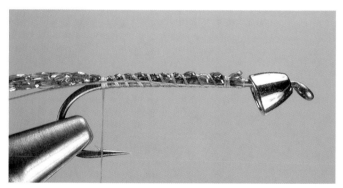

3. Pull the Sparkle Braid and the wire toward the rear of the hook as you wrap the thread back over both of them at the same time. Anchor the wire and the braid at the bend of the hook with several tight turns of thread.

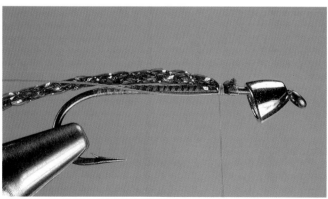

2. Tie in both the Sparkle Braid and the wire at about the 80 percent point on the hook. Be careful not to creep too far forward here so you will have enough room for the collar later.

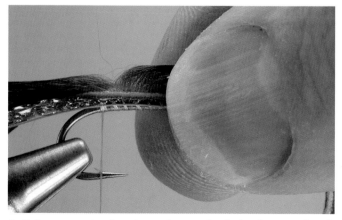

4. Select a squirrel strip and part the hair about a shank length from its end. Place this part in the hair above the tie-down point at the bend of the hook.

5. Tie the squirrel strip down in the part at the bend of the hook with a few tight turns of thread. Be sure to make these wraps right over the top of each other to create less bulk at the tie-down point.

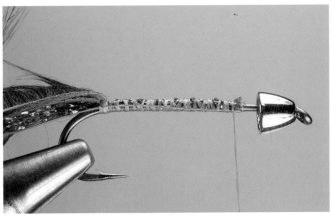

6. Pull the front end of the squirrel strip back out of the way (place it in your material spring on the vise, if you have one). Advance the thread to the starting point.

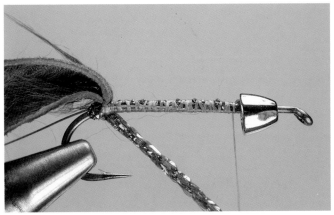

7. Take a single turn with the Sparkle Braid *under* the tail strip.

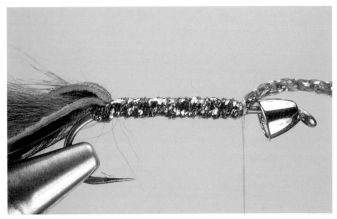

8. Continue wrapping the Sparkle Braid forward to make a smooth, level body. Tie the braid off at the starting point.

9. Pull the squirrel strip forward over the top of the body and part the hair at the starting point. Tie the hide down to the hook tightly, taking care to not trap any fur, just the hide.

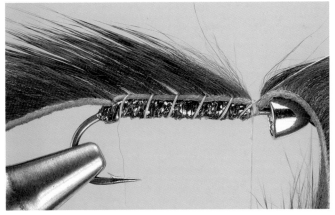

10. Evenly spiral wrap the wire forward through the squirrel strip wing. Part the hair at each segment and feed the wire down to the body, creating an evenly spaced rib. Tie the wire off at the starting point. Clip the excess wire.

11. Put the remaining end of the squirrel strip back into your material spring once again to hold it out of the way. Place a drop of Zap Gel into the back of the cone.

13. Shove the cone back onto the collar so the Zap Gel will take hold and lock everything in. Clip the thread. There is no need to whip-finish the thread, as the glue will hold everything in place under the cone.

12. Wrap the front end of the squirrel strip forward right up to and into the cone. Tie the strip off with a couple firm wraps of thread.

14. The finished fly.

PATTERN VARIATIONS

CHARLIE CRAVEN

SLUMPBUSTER
(Rust)

Hook:	Size 4–12 Tiemco 5263
Thread:	Black 70-denier Ultra Thread
Cone:	Gold tungsten, size 4–6 (large), size 8–10 (medium)
Rib:	Copper brown Ultra Wire (Brassie)
Body:	Copper Sparkle Braid
Wing/Tail:	Rust pine squirrel
Collar:	Rust pine squirrel

CHARLIE CRAVEN

SLUMPBUSTER
(Natural)

Hook:	Size 4–12 Tiemco 5263
Thread:	Black 70-denier Ultra Thread
Cone:	Gold tungsten size 4–6 (large), size 8–10 (medium)
Rib:	Blue Ultra Wire (Brassie)
Body:	Royal blue Sparkle Braid
Wing/Tail:	Black pine squirrel
Collar:	Black pine squirrel

CHARLIE CRAVEN

SLUMPBUSTER
(Black)

Hook:	Size 4–12 Tiemco 5263
Thread:	Black 70-denier Ultra Thread
Cone:	Gold tungsten size 4–6 (large), size 8–10 (medium)
Rib:	Blue Ultra Wire (Brassie)
Body:	Royal blue Sparkle Braid
Wing/Tail:	Black pine squirrel
Collar:	Black pine squirrel

CHAPTER 19

Bouface

Colorado has some excellent pike fisheries—among them the Williams Fork, Elevenmile, Stage Coach, and Sanchez reservoirs—and this fly was originally designed for pike. I needed to create a fly that looked big and enticing in the water, but was relatively easy to cast. The first Bouface rolled off the vise around 1980, its name inspired by the fly's marabou collar.

My first pike trip was to Williams Fork Reservoir outside of Kremmling, Colorado. I was armed with an 8-weight and a box of Boufaces. I had read that northern pike liked the color combination of yellow and black, so that is what I tied on. The pattern had a black rabbit fur Zonker strip tail and a yellow marabou collar. I knew the reservoir had lots of northern pike in it, but having never fished for them, I had no game plan. I arrived at the reservoir and parked at the first place I could park, suited up, and walked down to a little bay. I had zero confidence. I cast as far as I could and retrieved the fly with steady long strips. The first pike I ever caught on a fly looked like a hand grenade that blew up in the water, with a brilliant flash of gold in the middle of the explosion. The fish made a long run and put up a ferocious battle that lasted about ten minutes. I was hooked on pike.

I was a pike fishing addict for about fifteen years, catching many like that first one (25 pounds on a chatillion scale). But, like most things, word got out, and it became difficult to hook pike over 10 pounds because they became conditioned to flies. After the Colorado reservoirs had been pounded for a few years, catching small pike and getting follows from adult pike didn't justify throwing an 8-weight fly rod all day, so I quit fishing for them in the late 1990s.

Those first Boufaces for pike were tied on a variety of hooks. When Tiemco introduced the 8089 Stinger hook that was all I used. The wire on the hook is thinner than a heavy wire saltwater hook, and the thin wire penetrates better. I have never had one fail. On a size 2 I have caught pike to 29 pounds and a 7 ½-pound bass on a size 10. My retrieve varied from a hand twist, to a

CHARLIE CRAVEN

BOUFACE
(Black)

Hook:	Size 4–10 Tiemco 200R
Bead:	Nickel brass bead
Thread:	Black 6/0 Danville
Wing/Tail:	Black pine squirrel
Flash:	Pearl Flashabou
Collar:	Black marabou
Head:	Black pine squirrel dubbing

steady strip, to ripping it in a fast as I could. All retrieves were at times productive, but I was never sure which retrieve was most effective. I just changed up whenever I felt like it.

The Bouface was also effective for largemouth bass. I think of the Bouface as the fly equivalent of the plastic worm, which for over fifty years has been one of the most successful bass baits of all time. The plastic worm looks like no forage that bass feed on, but its action is so enticing that bass can't help themselves. I wanted a pattern that, when retrieved, would pulsate and undulate and suggest something alive. There are no better materials than rabbit and marabou to achieve this effect.

My initial Boufaces were tied in many of the popular pike and bass color combinations, but I finally settled on all black, chartreuse, black and yellow, and red and white. Red and white Boufaces have proven to be an effective lake trout pattern. If I could have only one color it would be black. I have caught my largest Colorado pike (29 pounds) and largemouth bass (9 pounds) on all-black Boufaces.

I started out fishing the pattern with no weight and a floating line. I then tried fishing the pattern with a size BB lead split shot pinched on the tippet right above the fly so that the fly dropped a little bit between strips. Warm- and coldwater fish can't resist a dropping fly. Adding split shot was so effective that I seldom fished the fly without it. When beads and cones came along, I stopped using shot to weight the fly. For those times when I want an unweighted version to fish above weedbeds or near the surface of the water, I forgo the bead or cone.

The Bouface was so effective for warmwater species I decided to try it for trout. I added a brass bead on the trout version because I knew I wouldn't need to suspend the fly over shallow weed beds like the bass and pike

John Burger with a monster pike caught on a Bouface in Elevenmile Reservoir, Colorado. LANDON MAYER

Though the Bouface was first designed for pike, it fast became an important pattern for trout in both flowing and still waters. This brown took an olive Bouface fished dead-drift. LANDON MAYER

A large brown in the "recovery room." JOHN BARR

versions. I tie the pattern on a 3XL streamer hook. For years I used the same rabbit as I did for the large versions, until I discovered pine squirrel Zonker strips, which have shorter hair fibers than rabbit and gave the fly better proportions. The pine squirrel exudes life in the water just like the rabbit.

You can cast and retrieve the Bouface like a standard streamer pattern, but I have had my most success dead-drifting it with or without an indicator. A friend of mine, who lives in New Zealand half of the year, tells me that dead-drifting an olive Bouface is his secret weapon for the crafty New Zealand trout. One tactic that I use for pressured stillwater trout is to fish the prevailing insect that is hatching, such as damselflies, midges, or *Callibaetis,* either slowly retrieved or fished under an indicator. After the hatch is finished, I fish an olive Bouface on a fast sinking or intermediate line (depending on the water depth) and trail a nymph representing whatever insect has been hatching. I use a 4- to 5-foot leader and tie my flies on with 3X fluorocarbon. I am not sure why the olive color is my most effective; it just is. I trail the nymph behind the Bouface with about 18 inches of tippet. I cast out and let the line sink the flies. Stay tight to your flies with a slow hand twist, as many grabs come on the drop. After you think your flies are at an appropriate depth (I start retrieving when it feels right—nothing scientific such as the countdown), retrieve with a fairly slow, one- to two-foot retrieve and strip set and lift the rod if a fish grabs one of the flies.

BOUFACE

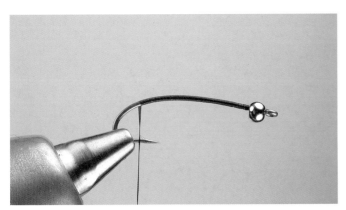

1. Slide the bead up to the hook eye. Insert the hook into the vise. Start the thread right behind the bead and wrap a smooth, tight thread base all the way back to the hook bend.

2. Part the hair on a squirrel strip with wet fingers. Place the parted section directly above the barb point and lash the hide down to the hook with several tight wraps of thread.

3. Lift the front end of the squirrel strip and move the thread forward to about an eye length back from the bead. Part the hair at this point and bind the hide down at the front.

4. Clip the excess pine squirrel as close to the hook as you can.

5. Tie two long strands of Flashabou in at the center of its length just behind the bead.

6. Pull two strands of flash back along the near side of the hook so they flank the squirrel strip, and bind them in place with two turns of thread. Pull the other two strands back along the far side and bind them in place.

7. Select a bushy marabou feather and measure it against the shank so the tips extend back to the barb on the hook.

8. Grasp the marabou at the pre-measured point . . .

9. and bind it down on the top of the hook with two turns of thread. Let the thread tension distribute the marabou around the top half of the hook. You may need to push the marabou around the shank to distribute it evenly.

10. Measure another clump of marabou to match the length of the first.

11. Tie the second clump in on the bottom of the shank in the same way as the first. Let this clump roll all the way around the bottom half of the hook shank.

12. Trim the butt ends of both marabou clumps as close to the hook as you can.

13. Wrap a smooth thread base over the remaining butts of the marabou right behind the bead.

14. Pull some fur from a squirrel strip and dub it onto the thread. Build up a small collar of dubbing right behind the bead to cover the marabou tie-off area. Whip-finish right behind the bead and clip the thread.

15. Trim the squirrel strip wing/tail so it extends one shank length beyond the hook bend. Trim the flash so it is just a hair longer than the squirrel.

16. Bouface when wet.

PATTERN VARIATIONS

BOUFACE
(Brown)

Hook:	Size 4–10 Tiemco 200R
Bead:	Gold brass bead
Thread:	Brown 6/0 Danville
Wing/Tail:	Brown pine squirrel
Flash:	Gold Flashabou
Collar:	Brown marabou
Head:	Brown pine squirrel dubbing

BOUFACE
(Olive)

Hook:	Size 4–10 Tiemco 200R
Bead:	Gold brass bead
Thread:	Olive 6/0 Danville
Wing/Tail:	Olive pine squirrel
Flash:	Gold Flashabou
Collar:	Olive marabou
Head:	Olive pine squirrel dubbing

CHAPTER 20

Meat Whistle

Bass fishing has been a passion of mine for over thirty years and I spend about seventy-five days a year fishing for them, mostly in my ponds, which contain both largemouth and smallmouth. I fish both conventional and fly tackle for bass, often alternating between the two. I'll kick along in my float tube with a casting rod on one side and a fly rod on the other, and whatever my mood or the situation dictates, use one or the other.

I like the hum of a level-wind casting reel and the challenge of skipping a jig under low hanging tree branches, but I am a fly fisherman at heart. I decided to try to design a pattern that would fish like the deadly jig and trailer that so many bass anglers love. In 2002 I started working on one. After a few years of trial and error I had it. I called it the Meat Whistle because it just seemed to call in the largest fish. It had roughly the same sink rate as my jig and trailer and was every bit as effective, if not more so at times.

For two spring seasons I fished the Meat Whistle and the jig and trailer head to head by switching off between the two after every fish. I was thrilled. The Meat Whistle caught the same size and amount of fish as the jig and trailer. In fact, at times the fly caught more big fish than the jig and trailer. I was ecstatic that I had designed a fly that could fish head to head with one of the most lethal bass lures ever.

My three favorite jig and trailer colors are watermelon (olive), pumpkinseed (rust), and black and blue, and those are the three colors of Meat Whistles I tie. I tied the pattern on a Gamakatsu jig hook using a cone for the weight. Lead eyes tend to collect weeds and the cone just made a better-looking pattern. I incorporated the life-exuding properties of rabbit and marabou, adding Sili Legs and some Flashabou. The pattern flat out caught bass as well as many other species of fish that like crawdads, including trout.

I usually fish the pattern on a 4- to 6-weight rod, depending on the wind. I use a Rio floating Clouser line, which has a taper that turns over the fly nicely, and a 9-foot leader tapered to 0X. I will cut off the regular monofilament 0X portion and add a couple feet of 0X

CHARLIE CRAVEN

MEAT WHISTLE
(Rust)

Hook:	Size 3/0–1/0 Gamakatsu 90 degree jig hook
Cone:	Copper, size 3/0 (large), size 2/0 (medium), size 1/0 (small)
Thread:	Rusty brown 140-denier Ultra Thread
Ribbing:	Copper brown Ultra Wire (Brassie)
Body:	Copper Diamond Braid
Wing:	Rust rabbit strip
Legs:	Pumpkin barred Sili Legs
Flash:	Copper Flashabou
Collar:	Brown marabou

fluorocarbon. I use a floating line because it gives me more options on my presentation than a sink tip or sinking line. With a sink tip or sinking line, and a sinking fly, you are pretty much limited to casting and stripping. A significant percentage of the takes occur when the fly is sinking with no retrieve. Watch the end of your fly line, as if you were nymph-fishing, for signals of a take. If the line tip moves, it is probably a fish eating your fly. Bass will hold onto this fly for a while before rejecting it, so it must feel fairly lifelike to them. Often you just get tight while the fly is sinking, in which case you strip set and lift the rod at the same time. You will either have wood or a bass. If you get no takers on the drop, hop the fly a couple times and let it sit. (The fly sits tail up and all the materials slowly undulate, which bass have a hard time resisting.) After you let it sit, you can shake it a little and start a hopping retrieve. Let the bass tell you the speed with which to retrieve it. A good rule of thumb is the colder the water, the slower you work your fly. The Meat Whistle can be hopped, slowly dragged, allowed to sit for as long as your patience allows, then shaken and hopped, or you can swim it like a regular streamer.

The Meat Whistle imitates a crawdad (also called crayfish or crawfish, depending on what part of the country you are from), one of the favorite foods of bass. They live in both coldwater and warmwater habitats and provide one of the highest nutritional values of all forage sources. Many crawdad patterns have prominent claws; however, bass prefer crawdads with small claws or no claws. The guides that fish with live crawdads pinch off the claws. When a crawdad is swimming or fleeing a predator they are hydrodynamic, with their claws held together behind them as their flipper tail propels them. (Actually, the claws are in front of them, but they swim backwards so we can say they are behind them.)

Bass are not the only fish that eat crawdads. All fish, both warm and coldwater species, love them. If their mouth is big enough to eat crawdads, they will not pass one up. Crawdads are found in many still and flowing water environments. Crawdads forage at night, so you

Bass fishing is a passion of mine, and I often fish with conventional gear. I designed the Meat Whistle—a fly named for its ability to call in big fish—to match the fish-catching ability of the popular bass lure, the jig and trailer.
CHARLIE MEYERS

Sometimes you need to add extra weight to even a heavy fly. To catch this nice rainbow, I added one large split-shot just up from the fly.
LANDON MAYER

The Meat Whistle probably imitates a bunch of different foods fish feed on, but I think trout take the rust-colored one for a crayfish.
LANDON MAYER

don't often see them, but fish have good night vision and see lots of them where they are present. It is a good pattern for larger trout. I have caught many large trout on the pattern, including a double-digit rainbow. A good friend of mine, T. L. Laurerman, who works for Wapsi in Mt. Home, Arkansas, sent me a photo of a heavy 31-inch brown that he caught on a Meat Whistle in the Norfork River. When traveling or spooked, sculpin hop along the bottom just like crawdads, so the Meat Whistle can be easily taken as a sculpin as well.

Another good friend, Landon Mayer, was fishing a reservoir in fall 2005 for staging browns, which are fish milling about at the inlet to the reservoir waiting for an increase in water flow to trigger their spawning run upstream. He did catch some nice browns but whacked a bunch of big carp that blew into his backing. Big carp love crawdads. Mike Atwell, another good friend, returned from a peacock bass trip in the spring of 2006 and told me the rust-colored Meat Whistle outfished the traditional peacock bass flies three to one. This pattern has accounted for big bluegill, crappie, smallmouth bass, channel catfish, and some Colorado pike up to 26 pounds.

Carp love crayfish, and that may be one reason that a Meat Whistle hopped along the bottom is a deadly fly for this fun fly-rod fish. LANDON MAYER

MEAT WHISTLE

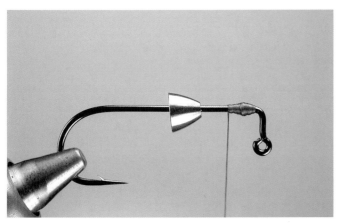

1. Place the cone on the hook and put the hook in the vise with the point down. Start the tying thread in front of the cone.

   Build up a small football-shaped nub of thread directly behind the right angle in the shank.

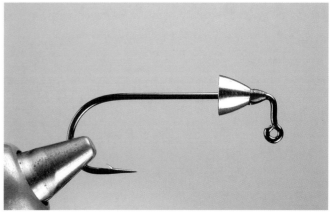

4. Shove the cone up tight against the nub of thread while the epoxy is still wet.

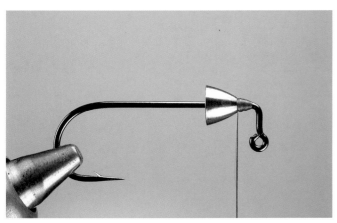

2. Push the cone up against the nub of thread and continue wrapping the thread to build it up so the nub fits tightly into the front of the cone.

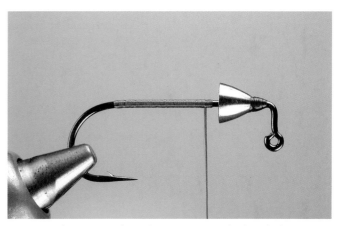

5. Start the tying thread once again behind the cone. Wrap a base of thread back to the bend of the hook and return the thread to just behind the cone.

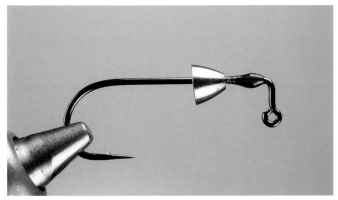

3. Slide the cone back, whip-finish and clip the thread. Apply a thin coat of epoxy or head cement to the thread nub.

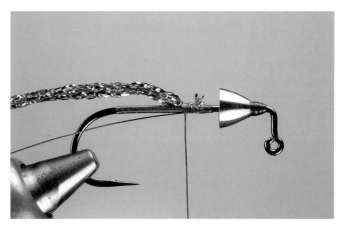

6. Tie in the copper braid and wire at the same time behind the cone.

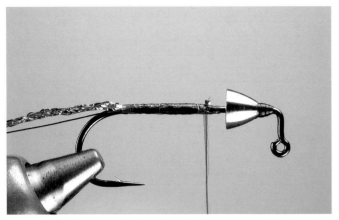

7. Wrap back over the braid and the wire to the bend of the hook. Return the thread to the front again.

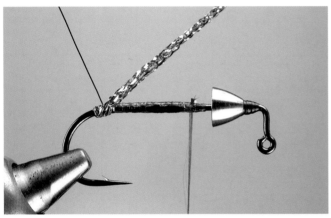

8. Make one turn of Sparkle Braid behind the wire, and then continue forward.

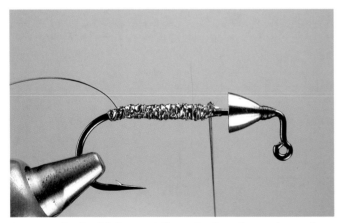

9. Wrap the braid forward from the bend, creating a slender body. Tie off the braid and clip the excess.

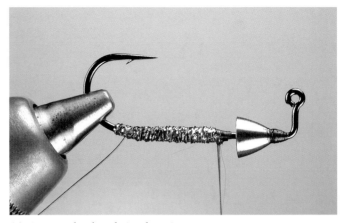

10. Invert the hook in the vise.

12. Pierce the strip of rabbit hide with the hook point right in the center of the strip. Make sure there is enough length for the strip to reach from the bend to the front of the hook.

13. Pull the hook through the hide and slide the strip down to the base of the body at the rear of the hook. This entails removing the hook from the vise to butt the strip up to the back of the body.

14. Tie the front end of the rabbit strip down tightly at the front edge of the body. Be careful not to build up too much bulk here. Clip the excess rabbit strip and cover the butt end with a smooth thread base.

15. Using the end of the wire like a needle, thread the tip of the wire through the rabbit strip Matuka-style wing. Keep the wire down close to the hook shank to keep from binding down the rabbit hair.

16. Continue ribbing the wire forward at evenly spaced intervals through the wing/body assembly as described above. Once at the front of the body, wrap the wire around the shank two times and tie it off with the thread. Clip the excess wire flush.

17. Turn the hook over in the vise once again. I prefer to turn the hook point down as much as possible, as this hook is wickedly sharp and will draw blood in the upright position.

18. Double over two strands of Sili Legs and loop them over the shank at the front edge of the body.

19. Tie the Sili Legs in place with a few tight turns of thread. They should be tied on top of the rabbit strip, along the sides of the fly. You should now have two legs on each side of the fly as shown.

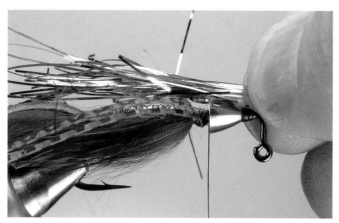

20. Move the thread forward, off the stub end of the rabbit hide and onto the bare shank behind the cone. Cut a small clump of Flashabou from the shank and tie it in behind the cone at the center of its length. The flash should extend about ½ inch past the hook bend.

21. Work the flash all the way around the shank with your fingers so it is evenly distributed 360 degrees around the shank. Double the long front ends back so they point to the rear of the hook and bind all the flash in place with several tight turns of thread.

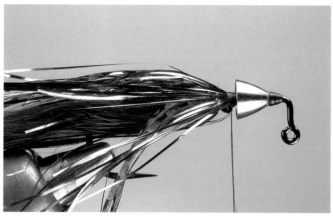

22. Wet your fingers and stroke the Flashabou back so it lies closely along the sides of the fly.

23. Select and measure a marabou feather so the tips reach back just past the bend of the hook.

24. Tie the marabou feather down at the back edge of the cone on the top of the hook shank. Try to spread the feather out so it encompasses the top half of the shank. Do not cut the butt end of the marabou yet.

25. Invert the hook and tie in another marabou feather on the bottom of the shank equaling the length of the first.

26. Maneuver the marabou around the shank so it encircles the hook. This can be done by pulling with your fingers and using the thread wraps to help "spin" the marabou around the hook.

27. Clip the butt ends of the marabou as close to the shank as possible. It is imperative to keep a clean tie down here to eliminate bulk.

28. Cover the butt ends of the marabou with a few tight, smooth wraps of thread. Pull a bit of fur from a spare rabbit strip. Mix this fur into a dubbing and twist it onto the thread. Build a small collar of dubbing covering the marabou tie-down area behind the cone. The dubbing should fill in the back of the cone as well. Whip-finish and clip the thread at the very back edge of the bead. Turn the hook over in the vise one last time. Pull the rabbit strip tail forward over the eye of the hook and trim the hide even with the front of the hook, leaving a shank-length long tail.

Trim the Sili Legs so they reach to about the middle of the tail.

29. The finished fly.

PATTERN VARIATIONS

CHARLIE CRAVEN

CHARLIE CRAVEN

MEAT WHISTLE (Olive)		MEAT WHISTLE (Black)	
Hook:	Size 3/0–1/0 Gamakatsu 90 degree jig	**Hook:**	Size 3/0–1/0 Gamakatsu 90 degree jig
Cone:	Gold, size 3/0 (large), size 2/0 (medium), size 1/0 (small)	**Cone:**	Black, size 3/0 (large), size 2/0 (medium), size 1/0 (small)
Thread:	Olive or black 140-denier Ultra Thread	**Thread:**	Black 140-denier Ultra Thread
Ribbing:	Chartreuse Ultra Wire (Brassie)	**Ribbing:**	Blue Ultra Wire (Brassie)
Body:	Olive Diamond Braid	**Body:**	Blue Diamond Braid
Wing:	Olive rabbit strip	**Wing:**	Black rabbit strip
Legs:	Barred olive Sili Legs	**Legs:**	Black with blue flake Sili Legs
Flash:	Holographic gold Flashabou	**Flash:**	Black holographic Flashabou
Collar:	Olive marabou	**Collar:**	Black marabou

Fly Combos

Over the years, I have fine-tuned my favorite combinations of flies that help me catch more fish. Multiple-fly rigs not only increase my catch rate by having more flies on the water, but they also help me figure out what the fish are eating or what stage of a hatching insect fish are keying in on.

Fishing several flies at a time is nothing new. Wet-fly fishermen have used this technique for centuries. But this approach applies to many more patterns than just a "cast" (a term used to describe a series of wet flies) of wets. I fish multiple-fly rigs with streamers, tandem dry flies, dry flies with droppers, and nymphs under an indicator.

Where I fish in the West, the most important mayflies are Blue-Winged Olives (*Baetis*), Pale Morning Duns (PMDs), and Tricos. Most of the other mayflies that hatch throughout the season are unpredictable or short-lived. Even though I won't be specifically talking about hatches other than *Baetis*, PMDs, and Tricos, you can use these techniques to fish other hatches in the East or West.

TWO DUNS

Fishing two dun patterns at the same time is useful if you want to increase your chances that a fish will see your fly (for example, inaccurate casting or cruising fish) or you want to fish different dun patterns to figure out which pattern they prefer. I fish a fly that's hard to see—because of poor light or the fly is small—behind an easy-to-see indicator pattern.

In riffle water, Hoppers or Stimulators work well as indicator flies, but when fishing in flatter water for crafty fish you want to use a less obtrusive, more imitative indicator fly. There are a number of good choices for visible dry flys that blend in with the hatch, such as various-sized Parachute Adams tied with high-visibility parachute posts made from brightly colored poly yarn. I tie a pattern called the Vis-A-Dun in *Baetis*, PMD, and Trico colors (see chapter 14). This fly is easy to see on the water even in bad light, sits well on the water, floats great, and is durable. During insect hatches, this pattern also catches its share of fish.

DRY PLUS AN EMERGER

Often during a hatch, fish feed on several stages of the emerging insect: emergers, cripples, or duns. I often use a PMD or *Baetis* Vis-A-Dun as my first fly and a floating or sunken emerger as my second. I tie the floating emerger on the Tiemco 101 (a light-wire, standard shank); the sunken pattern on a 2488H (heavy wire, short-shank, wide gap).

For a PMD or *Baetis* hatch, I generally fish a Vis-A-Dun trailed by a floating or sunken Flashback Barr Emerger. For small *Baetis*, I use a Micro-Emerger. The floating emerger also doubles as a cripple imitation.

DRY PLUS SUNKEN SPINNER

Baetis hatch in Colorado from March through November. On cloudy days in the spring and fall anglers can see bank-to-bank hatches.

With these heavy *Baetis* hatches, I always wondered why I never saw an equally heavy spinner fall. After talking with Mike Lawson last fall (whose book *Spring Creeks* is one of the most important angling books ever written), I finally learned the *Baetis* spinner-fall mystery. According to Mike, many *Baetis* spinners do not fall on the surface of the river (some do), but most of them crawl from the bank into the river or dive into the river and lay their eggs underwater. The males often accompany the females.

Fish a larger, more visible dry fly to help you track the smaller one.

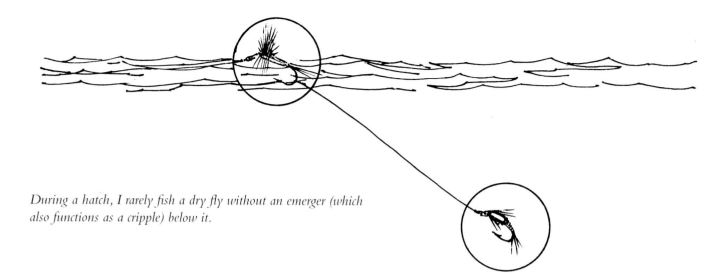

During a hatch, I rarely fish a dry fly without an emerger (which also functions as a cripple) below it.

When indicator nymphing or fishing a wet fly below a dry fly, a *Baetis* spinner is a good choice for your bottom fly if there has been *Baetis* activity.

Most anglers do not think of fishing spinners as nymphs; however, this is a good technique whenever there has been any spinner activity. Sunk spinners are not only good for *Baetis,* but they also work for PMD hatches. If trout are rising to PMD spinners, I use a PMD Vis-A-Dun with a sunken PMD spinner dropper.

Fishing sunken spinners is my main technique for hooking fish during a Trico spinner fall when fish are rising to Trico spinners. Tricos, which start hatching in Colorado in early July and can last into October, are the most dependable hatch and spinner fall in the West. Trout become accustomed to Trico spinner falls and love to eat them, long after they quit rising to them.

However, fishing floating Trico spinner patterns can be frustrating. Your fly competes with lots of naturals and even accurate casters have to cast many times before a hookup. I like to use a Trico Vis-A-Dun as the first fly and drop a Drowned Trico spinner off the bend. The Trico Vis-A-Dun is not a classic Trico spinner imitation, but it has a black body and at the right angle trout will take it as a spinner. Its main purpose is to act as an indicator for the sunken spinner. When fishing a drowned spinner, you can often fish a larger fly, which makes it easier to land larger fish. I tie the fly on a Tiemco 2488H hook (3X-wide gap, 2XS shank, heavy-wire hook), which allows me to tie a small fly with excellent hooking capabilities. With the heavy wire, I can also put a lot of pressure on larger fish and land them quickly. The Antron wings glow when the sun is on them, which allows the trout to easily spot the fly, and the Quick Descent dubbing thorax helps sink the fly.

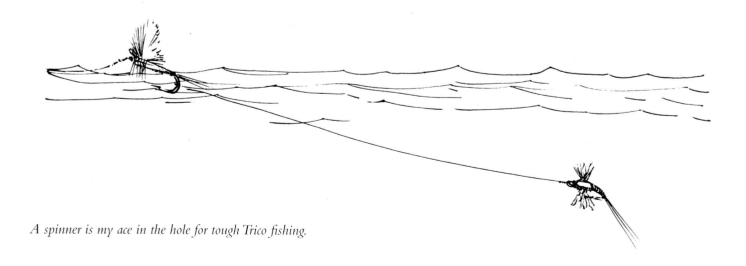

A spinner is my ace in the hole for tough Trico fishing.

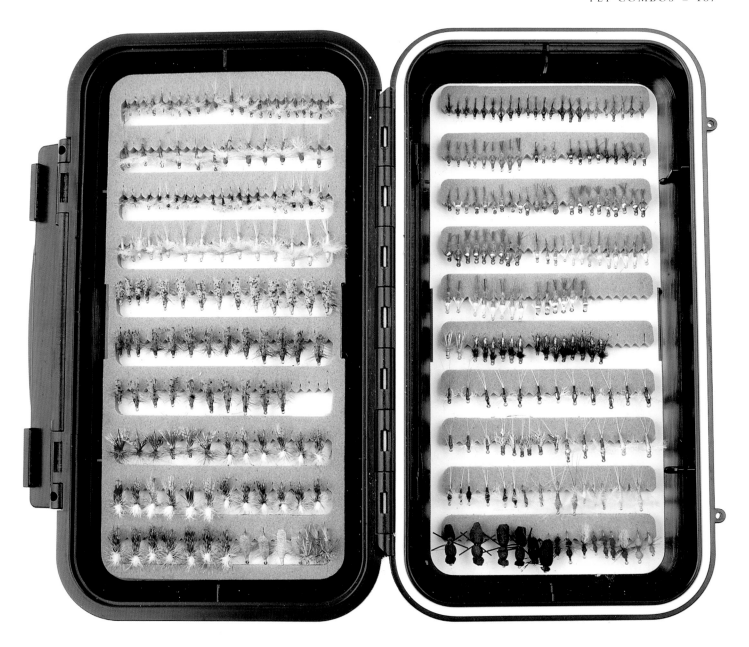

Side 1 of my hatch box (for when I encounter rising fish) holds hatch-matching drys for the major mayfly, caddis, and stonefly species that I encounter most. For Vis-A-Duns, I carry Baetis (#18–26, rows 1–2), Tricos (#18–24, row 3), and PMDs (#16–20, row 4). For caddis adults, I carry Web Wing Caddis in sizes 16–20 in tan (row 5), brown (row 6), and dark dun (row 7) and Lawson's Spent-Winged Caddis and E-Z Caddis (#16–18, rows 8–10). I also always have a few Yellow Sallies on hand (#16–18, row 10). I like to use a Web Wing or Spent-Winged Caddis trailed behind the easy-to-see E-Z Caddis.

Side 2 of this fly box holds the emerger, pupa, or spinner stages of the adults on side 1, plus one row of beetles and ants. Micro Emergers (#20–24, row 1) imitate small Baetis or midge pupae; Baetis Barr Emergers (#16–24, rows 2–3) in different versions are great choices as a bottom fly in a nymph or HCD setup at any time of the year; and PMD Barr Emergers (#16–18, rows 4–5) in both floating and sinking versions do double duty as both Pale Morning Dun and yellow sally imitations. I fish green Graphic Caddis Pupae (#14–18, row 6) in spring and summer, and tan in the fall, often under a Vis-A-Dun that matches mayfly activity. For spinner falls, I fish sunken spinners and carry Trico, Baetis, and PMD versions (#16–24, rows 7–9). My best rig for Trico spinner falls is a B/C Hopper, #18 black Copper John, and #20–24 Trico Sunken Spinner. For bank feeders during non-hatch situations, I'll often fish a beetle or ant (row 10). DAVID SIEGFRIED/FLY FISHERMAN

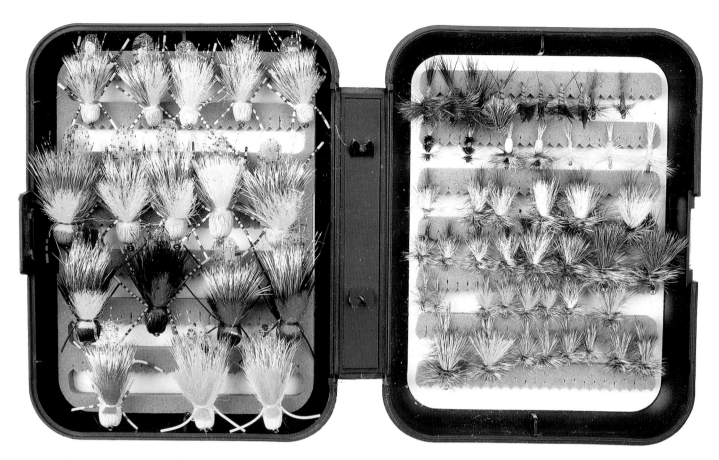

Side 1 of my hopper and miscellaneous dry-fly box holds various colors of B/C Hoppers (#6–10). Side 2 holds Mahogany Duns and Green Drakes (row 1), attractors such as Royal Wulffs and Humpies (row 2), and Stimulators (rows 3–6). These high-floating visible flies are all great for suspending nymphs and emergers. DAVID SIEGFRIED/FLY FISHERMAN

OTHER DEADLY COMBOS

YELLOW SALLIES

Yellow Stimulator plus floating PMD Emerger in the film. Most stoneflies crawl out onto the bank to hatch, but yellow sallies hatch in the film just like PMDs. In Colorado, PMDs and yellow sallies often hatch at the same time, so this combination covers a lot of bases.

MIDGES

Baetis or Trico Vis-A-Dun (Sizes 22–24) plus a size 20 or smaller Micro-Emerger or Flashback *Baetis* Emerger (an excellent midge imitation).

CADDIS

Lawson's E-Z Adult Caddis plus Barr's Graphic Caddis Pupa (tan or olive covers most caddis hatches). Either dead-drift the flies or swing them into the riseform.

BEETLES AND ANTS

Vis-A-Dun (color to match any mayflies on the water) plus beetle or ant. My favorite beetle is a size 16 Mike Lawson's Foam Beetle without a bright indicator top. I don't like indicators on beetles because if they don't land upright the orange post can spook fish.

Side 1 of my nymph box holds various colors of Copper Johns and variations. Side 2 holds Tung Teasers (#12–18, row 1), Net Spinner Caddis Larvae (#14–16, row 2)—which I've simplified in my current box to versions of the Cased and Uncased Caddis Larvae—Golden Tungstones (#10–18, row 3), Dark Tungstones (#6–10, row 4), Cranefly Larvae (#8–10, row 5), various aquatic worms (#8–14, row 6), various egg patterns (#10–16, row 7), and Pure Midge Larvae (#18–24, row 8).

DAVID SIEGFRIED/FLY FISHERMAN

My basic leader setup for all of these dry-plus-dropper combinations is a 9-foot, 4X leader to which I add 12 inches of 5X and, if necessary, another 36 inches of 6X for Tricos or Baetis. I add the second fly with 6 to 10 inches of 5X or 6X fluorocarbon tippet tied to the bend of the first fly.

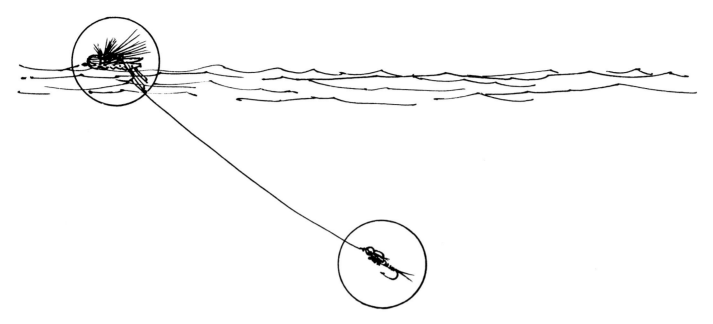

When there are no rising trout, fishing a Copper John behavior a B/C Hopper is one of my favorite approaches, spring through fall. For a leader I use a 6-foot weight-forward Umpqua leader or a standard 7 ½-foot leader tapered to 3X (the lightest tippet that will turn the Hopper and trailing fly over effectively). I use five-turn clinch knots for all the connections and attach the Copper John to a 1- to 4-foot section of 4X fluorocarbon behind the Hopper.

My basic leader setup for all of these dry-plus-dropper combinations is a 9-foot, 4X leader to which I add 1 foot of 5X and, if necessary, another 2 ½ feet of 6X for Tricos or *Baetis*. I add the second fly with 6–10 inches of a 5X or 6X fluorocarbon tippet tied to the bend of the first fly.

HOPPER COPPER COMBO

When there are no rising trout, fishing a Copper John behind a buoyant B/C Hopper is one of my favorite approaches spring through fall. The Copper John sinks rapidly and is an effective pattern on its own. You can also add a third fly to this rig, dropped off the bend of the Copper, that imitates the prevailing natural such as a *Baetis* or PMD nymph or emerger. But to get used to the technique of casting and fishing multiple flies at one time, you may just want to start with two flies.

For a leader I use a 6-foot weight-forward Umpqua leader or a standard 7 ½-foot leader tapered to 3X (the lightest tippet that will turn the Hopper and trailing fly over effectively). I use five-turn clinch knots for all the connections and attach a Copper John to a 1- to 4-foot section of 4X fluorocarbon behind the Hopper.

DOUBLE STREAMERS

When I fish streamers, I generally fish two at a time. There are numerous combinations of streamers that can be effective. The main principles I follow are to use different size, color, action, and silhouette combinations until I figure out the patterns that work best together. I often fish a smaller Bouface behind a Slumpbuster or fish two Slumpbusters tied with tungsten-cone heads. The Slumpbuster has a baitfish silhouette when it is wet and has been my most productive streamer over the years. My favorite combination is a natural pine squirrel Slumpbuster as the first fly followed by a rust, olive, or black Slumpbuster one or two sizes smaller.

When fishing this combination, casting to the banks and stripping or casting and swinging the fly work well. My favorite technique when fishing from a boat is to rip these streamers through shallow water and then pause my retrieve and let the streamers drop through deep holes, drop-offs, channels, depressions, and behind rocks. Large trout love to take this fly on the drop. The long leader and floating line are sometimes more awkward to cast than a sinking-tip line, but I like the ability to mend and control the fly to fish it though both shallow and deep water.

The flies in this small box catch my largest fish. I carry only three streamer patterns, but make sure I have a range of colors, weights, and sizes. I like to carry unweighted (or lightly weighted) Slumpbusters (side 1, top left) and heavily weighted patterns (side 2, bottom right) to cover a range of water depths. I also carry Meat Whistles with dumbbell eyes (sides 1 and 2, top) and tungsten cones (side 2, right). Boufaces in olive, black, and brown (side 1, bottom) round out my selection. DAVID SIEGFRIED/FLY FISHERMAN

For most of my streamer fishing I use a floating line, but at times I'll use a sinking-tip line with a 4- to 6-foot leader tapered to 0X. When streamer fishing with a floating line, I like to use an Umpqua 9-foot weight-forward leader tapered to 0X. Attach your first fly with a clinch knot. I attach my second fly with about 2 feet of 0X.

CASTING TIP

When casting multiple-fly rigs, it's important to use the right leader and tippet configurations. Once you have that set, all you have to do is modify your casting and you shouldn't have too many problems with tangles. Remember to accelerate your back and forward casts (like you should on every cast) and to use a wide casting loop.

INDEX OF FLY PATTERNS